FIGHTING MACHINES

OF WORLD WAR II

First published in the UK 1984 by Blandford Press, Link
House, West Street, Poole, Dorset BH15 1LL

Copyright © 1984 Blandford Press Ltd.

Distributed in the United States by Sterling Publishing
Co., Inc., 2 Park Avenue, New York, N.Y. 10016

British Library Cataloguing in Publication Data

White, B. T.
  Fighting machines of World War 2.
  1. Tanks (Military science)—History—
  Pictorial works   2. World War, 1939-1945—
  Tank warfare—Pictorial works   3. Artillery
  —History—20th century—Pictorial works
  4. World War, 1939-1945—Campaigns—Pictorial
  works
  I. Title   II. Bowers, Michael
  623.74′752′09044   UG446.5

ISBN 0 7137 1452 2

Typeset in 8/9 Rockwell Light by Megaron
Typesetting.

Printed in Hong Kong by Lee-Fung Asco Printers

Contents

Introduction

This book presents a fascinating collection of the tanks, armoured vehicles and artillery which were used by the powers in World War II. The armouries of Britain, France, USA, USSR, Germany and Italy are well represented by the illustrations which reveal an extraordinary range of firepower.

Represented in the book are not only the great successes of the War – the Tiger tanks, the T34s and so on – but also many of the strange inventions which were complete failures. There are also a number of interesting developments which arrived too late to be used in action.

The extent of the inventiveness and ingenuity employed by designers on both sides of the conflict emerges with great clarity. Some of these men had no military experience, or very little, but were able, nevertheless, to design fighting vehicles which have taken their places in history.

The emphasis in this volume is on vehicles rather than artillery. The more important and successful guns are illustrated, but artillery is an immense subject in its own right and could fill a larger book than this. Rather what we have tried to do is present a balanced view of the *development* that was achieved by these six powers during the period 1939-45, rather than gather together a catalogue of everything that was available to them.

Renault Char Moyen D.2

Direct in line of descent from the light Renault FT of 1917 through the NC 27 and NC 31 (sold abroad but not used by France), the Char D.2 was one of the first modern types of infantry medium tanks to be supplied to the French Army after the First World War.

The Renault-designed D.2 had a rear-mounted engine – a six-cylinder Renault of 150 h.p. – with transmission via a four-speed gearbox to rear sprockets. The crew compartment and turret were set fairly well forward, the cast turret mounting a 47-mm. gun and one 7.5-mm. machine-gun. Armour was to a maximum of 40-mm. and the top speed was 15 m.p.h. The suspension, protected by hinged side skirting plates, consisted on each side of three bogie units of four road wheels and sprung on vertical coil springs. Additionally there were single road wheels each side in front of and behind the bogie groups. First appearing in 1933, the Char D.2 was largely superseded by the Char B series by 1940. Nevertheless, the D.2 still remained in first-line service and formed part of the equipment of General de Gaulle's 4e Division Cuirassée.

Renault Chars de Bataille B.1 and B.1 bis

Chars B represented the principal striking force of the four French armoured divisions (Divisions Cuirassées – D.C.R.) that were in existence by 15 May 1940 (the last, under the command of General de Gaulle, created on this day) and, as such, were perhaps the most significant Allied tanks of the era. Each of these divisions had an establishment of four battalions of combat tanks, organised by 1940 in a demi-brigade of two battalions of Chars B.1 bis and a demi-brigade of two battalions of much lighter tanks, in most cases H.39s.

The specification for the Char B had its origin as far back as 1921, but this was not agreed in a final form until 1926 and three prototypes were built between 1929 and 1931. From trials of these emerged the first production model, Char B.1, the earliest of which were completed about 1935.

The Char B showed the influence of the First World War traditions in its long, high profile, but its armour was good for its time, and it armament – a short 75-mm.

gun, a 47-mm. gun and two machine-guns – was powerful, although the heavy weapon was limited in use by its mounting low in the hull front. Mobility, too, was not neglected because a six-cylinder Renault engine of 250 h.p. gave a top speed of 17 m.p.h. Steering was by means of an advanced regenerative controlled differential system, by means of which also the 75-mm. gun, which had no independent traverse, could be laid.

The second production model, Char B.1 bis (all of which went to the four D.C.R.), had a 47-mm. turret gun model SA 35, with a longer barrel than the model SA 34 of the B.1, and a 300 h.p. engine which increased the overall performance generally and the top speed slightly, although the radius of action was reduced. The maximum armour protection of 40-mm. in B.1 was increased to 60-mm. in the B.1 bis.

Production of the Char B series was undertaken by Renault, Schneider, F.C.M., F.A.M.H. (Saint Chamond) and AMX and about 380 were built.

Renault Char Léger R.35

Designed and produced by the Renault company to replace its famous predecessor, the FT 17, the R.35 appeared in 1935. A two-man light tank of just under 10 tons, the R.35 was intended to re-equip the tank regiments supporting infantry divisions and, as such, had relatively heavy armour protection (to a maximum of 45-mm. – greater than that of many contemporary medium tanks of other countries), and a short-barrelled low-velocity 37-mm. gun with coaxial 7.5-mm. machine-gun. This was at the expense of mobility, because a speed of only 12 m.p.h. was attained with the Renault four-cylinder 82 h.p. engine.

The general layout of the R.35 was conventional, although the use of castings for the turret (pioneered in the Renault FT 17) and parts of the hull was uncommon outside France at the time. The rear-mounted engine drove sprockets at the front of the track and the suspension consisted, each side, of five road wheels and a low-mounted idler wheel at the rear. The road wheels were mounted in two articulated bogies, each of two wheels, and a single. The wheel movement was controlled by springs made up of horizontally mounted rubber washers.

Although production of the R.35 was insufficient completely to replace the FT 17 in the infantry tank regiments, this tank equipped twenty-three battalions and was an important element in the French rearmament programme: it was certainly one of the best-known tanks of its era. Some were also employed in the Divisions Cuirassées in lieu of H.39s.

An improved model of the R.35 had the longer-barrelled SA 38 37-mm. gun and a further development, known as R.40, had an entirely new suspension system designed by AMX with armoured skirting plates. This tank had a far better cross-country performance than the R.35 but only two battalions had been equipped with it by 1940.

Hotchkiss Char Légers H.35 and H.39

This light tank was produced at the same time as the Renault R.35 and was adopted by the cavalry, just as the R.35 was used to re-equip the tank units of the infantry.

The Renault and Hotchkiss tanks were rather alike in appearance and had identical armament of one 37-mm. gun and one 7.5-mm. machine-gun. The H.35, however, had the special characteristic required by the cavalry of a better speed and this was attained to some extent at the expense of armour protection, which was at a maximum of 34-mm. compared with the infantry tank's 45-mm. The Hotchkiss H.35 had a similar suspension system to the Renault's but using coil springs instead of rubber washers and with one extra road wheel each side: the longer-track base contributing to a better

performance cross-country at speed.

In the course of production of the H.35 the original Hotchkiss six-cylinder 75 h.p. engine was replaced by one of 120 h.p. and this increased the maximum speed from 17½ m.p.h. to 22½ m.p.h. The rear hull deck over the engine was higher in this model, known as H.39. Finally, the turret in the later H.39s to be produced was equipped with a long 37-mm. gun.

One of the most important types of French tank of its era, over 1,000 Hotchkiss H.35s and H.39s were produced and with the Somua S.35 they formed the backbone of the cavalry Divisions Légères Méchaniques (DLM) as well as subsequently equipping most of the light battalions in each of the Divisions Cuirassées (DCR) formed in 1939-40.

The Somua S.35 was regarded as the best French tank of the early part of the Second World War and, indeed, was considered by some as one of the best medium tanks of its era in the world. Certainly, after the surrender of France in 1940 this was one of the few types of French tank to be used by the Germans to equip some of their own tank units.

Produced by the Societé d'Outillage Méchanique et Usinage d'Artillerie (SOMUA), the S.35 first appeared in 1935. Intended for the mechanised cavalry, it was originally classified as an Automitrailleuse de Combat (AMC) but later was designated Char de Cavalerie and became one of the principal fighting vehicles of the Divisions Légères Méchaniques. Each of these mechanised cavalry divisions had one regiment (two squadrons) of S.35s in its tank brigade, together with a regiment of Hotchkiss H.39s.

The Somua S.35 shared a common turret design with the Char B.1 bis but had few other similarities with the heavier vehicle. The S.35 had a good road speed of 25

m.p.h. without undue sacrifice of armour protection, which was up to 55-mm., and although the hull was somewhat high the armour was rounded and well-shaped to a design facilitated by the cast form of manufacture used.

The armament of one 47-mm. gun and one 7.5-mm. machine-gun in an electrically traversed turret was as good as or better than that of the majority of German tanks in 1940, although the tank's performance in action was retarded by the fact that the commander was also the gunner.

Power was supplied by a Somua V-8 engine of 190 h.p. linked to a synchromesh five-speed gearbox which transmitted the drive to the tracks via rear sprockets. The steering was of the double differential type offering one radius of turn for each of the five forward gears. The suspension consisted of small road wheels in pairs sprung on leaf springs and protected by side armour skirting.

Renault A.M.C. 35 type ACG 1

This light combat cavalry tank ('Automitrailleuse de Combat') was one of the most advanced French tanks for its size in that as well as being equipped with a good gun it had a two-man turret – the first French tank to do so – with all the advantages in command it conferred.

Designed by Renault, the AMC 35 used suspension of similar design to that of the R.35, but the hull and turret were redesigned and used a bolted or riveted form of construction instead of cast. As required of a cavalry tank, a reasonably good maximum speed of 25 m.p.h. was attained, thanks to the satisfactory power/weight ratio conferred by the 180 h.p. Renault six-cylinder engine. The armament consisted of a 7.5-mm. machine-gun and either a 47-mm. gun (as shown in the pictures) or a high-velocity 25-mm. cannon.

Manufacture of the AMC 35 was undertaken by l'Atelier d'Issy les Moulineaux (AMX) and, somewhat surprisingly, for in retrospect this seems to have been one of the best pre-war French light tank designs, only 100 were built. Twelve tanks of this type were supplied to the Belgian Army.

Renault A.M.R. 35 type ZT

Designed by Renault for the French cavalry, this light tank was a battle reconnaissance vehicle in the category of 'Automitrailleuse de Reconnaissance' (AMR), to follow the earlier Renault model 33, type VM.

Known by its manufacturers as type ZT, the AMR 35 had the main characteristic demanded of this class of tank of high speed (37 m.p.h.), although at the expense of armour protection which was in the 5-13-mm. range. The armament was, however, an improvement over its predecessor in that the second model (shown in the illustrations) had a 13.2-mm. heavy machine-gun (in place of the 7.5-mm. machine-gun of the AMR 33 and first model of AMR 35). In the final model of AMR 35 a 25-mm. gun was fitted.

The mechanical layout of the AMR 35 was similar to that of most French light tanks of the period – a rear-mounted engine (four-cylinder Renault, 80 h.p.) with drive to front sprockets. The suspension consisted, each side, of one pair of road wheels and two singles controlled by rubber washers in compression – a system also used in the R.35 and H.35. The two-man crew occupied the centre part of the vehicle, the driver at the left. The turret was also at the left-hand side of the hull, the engine being at the right.

Nearly 200 of these tanks were built and many were still in service in 1939-40, although it was the intention to replace them with the slower but much better-protected Hotchkiss H.35.

This Automitrailleuse de Découverte, which was designed in 1933, first entered service with the French Army in 1935, and today still looks modern in appearance, was one of the best armoured cars of its kind in the world in the early part of the Second World War.

Known as the Panhard type 178 to its manufacturers and as AMD Panhard modèle 1935 by the French Army, this was the first four-wheeled, four-wheel-drive rear-engined armoured car to go into series production for a major country and the same layout was subsequently adopted by the United Kingdom, Germany, the United States and Italy, among others.

Power was provided by a four-cylinder Panhard-type S.K. engine of 105 h.p. and transmitted through a gearbox with four forward and four reverse speeds. The maximum speed was 45 m.p.h. The crew of four included a second driver at the rear, and a speed of 26 m.p.h. could be attained in reverse.

Early examples of the Panhard 178 had a short-calibre gun or, in some cases, two machine-guns but the standard armament was a 25-mm. high-velocity gun and one 7.5-mm. machine-gun mounted coaxially in the turret. A command version had a fixed structure replacing the turret and was without armament. The armour protection of the Panhard was in the range 20 mm. maximum and 7-mm. minimum.

The Panhard armoured cars were used by the mechanised cavalry for long-distance reconnaissance in the reconnaissance regiments of the Divisions Légères Méchaniques (D.L.M.), and in the so-called reconnaissance groups of infantry divisions (G.R.D.I.): in both types of unit they were grouped with cavalry full-tracked or half-tracked armoured vehicles. After the defeat of France in 1940, the Germans acknowledged the merit of the Panhard 178 by taking all those available into service in the German Army, where they received the designation of Pz. Spähwagen P.204(f).

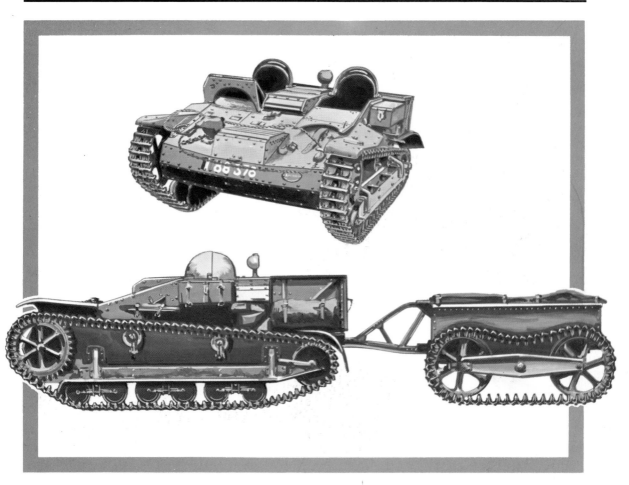

This small tracked vehicle was produced in large numbers from 1931 onwards as an armoured supply tractor for the French infantry. Weighing only about 2 tons, its own carrying capacity was slight, but a tracked trailer was normally towed. Both tractor and trailer were derived from Carden-Loyd designs and a very similar vehicle, the Carden-Loyd Mark VI, was widely used by the British Army in the 1930s although, unlike its French contemporary, it had been superseded by the outbreak of the Second World War.

Although a version of the Renault UE with a mounted machine-gun for the co-driver was built, the great majority were unarmed and intended purely as front-line supply vehicles. They were fully enclosed, with light armour protection up to a maximum of 7-mm. The trailer, which could carry about 500 kg, was open and unprotected, and could be used with or without tracks.

The Renault UE was powered by a four-cylinder Renault 35 h.p. engine mounted between the two members of the crew.

Built by Forges et Chantiers de la Mediterrannée in conjunction with Automobiles M. Berliet (which provided the engine) the FCM 36 came into production in 1936 to help increase the supply of tanks for the French infantry-support units. As such, it was a tank in the same broad specification as the more widely known Renault R.35, but the FCM 36 had some unusual features for French tanks of its time and some of these were in advance of developments elsewhere.

Of fairly conventional general layout, the FCM 36 had the engine at the rear, driving rear sprockets, but it was uncommon in that this was a diesel (of Ricardo design and built by Berliet under licence). Only two other French tanks produced around this time (the AMX 38 and B1 ter) shared this feature, which gave the FCM 36 a range of 200 miles – double that of most of its contemporaries in the French Army.

The armour protection was to the 40-mm. maximum standard required of French infantry tanks of this period, but another rare feature for the time was that for both hull and turret welded construction was used – an achievement which anticipated the method of welding armour plate in the United Kingdom, for example, by several years. The angles of the armour plate were (except for the suspension skirting plates) well thought out and the flat surfaces were able to offer the same sort of protection as the rounded cast armour that was used in most other French infantry tanks. The armament was one 37-mm. gun and one 7.5-mm. machine-gun.

Only 100 FMC 36s were built and this number, allowing for reserves, was sufficient for the equipment of two units – 4e and 7e Bataillons de Chars de Combat.

The French 155-mm. Schneider Howitzer M 1917,
also adopted by the US Army as their M 1917.
It remained in use until 1945.

The French Hotchkiss 25-mm. M39
Anti-aircraft gun, a great deal of
mounting for not much gun.

Over 500 of these light tanks and of the earlier model PzKpfw IA took part in the campaign in the West in 1940. Before this they had taken an even more prominent part in the Polish campaign. However, it had never been the intention of the German High Command, when these light-machine-gun-armed tanks were put into production, to employ them in major campaigns in this way.

When the expansion and re-equipment of the Reichswehr was decided on in 1932 the main need, initially, was for a supply of tanks that could be built cheaply and issued to the troops for training. For this purpose the firms of Krupp, MAN, Rheinmetall, Henschel and Daimler-Benz were asked to submit prototypes on the lines of the British Vickers-Carden-Loyd light tanks that, by then, had reached a fairly satisfactory state of mechanical development. The Krupp design known as L.K.A.1 was selected as the first production model in 1934, eventually becoming known as, PzKpfw IA. A second prototype, L.K.B.1, in which a more powerful engine (a Maybach Krupp air-cooled model) replaced the original Krupp air-cooled type, was also put into production as PzKpfw I, Ausf. B.

The earliest versions to appear of both these models had open-top hulls and no turrets. This, and the designation – landwirtschaftliche Schlepper (La.S.) (agricultural tractor) – was intended to disguise their true purpose, although in this form they were still entirely suitable for driver training and tactical exercises.

The layout of both the A and the B models was the same – a rear-mounted engine with the transmission led forward to front driving sprockets. The crew compartment was in the centre of the vehicle, with the driver at the left. The turret, mounting two machine-guns, was off-set to the right on the roof of the hull. In the suspension the front road wheel was sprung independently on a coil spring and the remaining wheels in pairs on leaf springs linked by a girder for extra rigidity.

In the PzKpfw IB an extra road wheel was added each side to carry the lengthened hull made necessary by the larger engine.

Production of the PzKpfw IA was limited to about 500, but nearly 2,000 of the IB, which was the much more important model, were built.

The six-wheeled German armoured cars in service in 1939-40 and used in the campaigns in Poland and the West were the product of experiments begun ten years earlier with standard six-wheeled lorry chassis.

In the late twenties, the most effective way of obtaining a reasonable cross-country performance without excessive cost was to use a six-wheeled lorry with drive transmitted to all four rear wheels. The commercial vehicle manufacturers of Daimler-Benz, Büssing and C.D. Magirus all made available chassis of this type and, with some modifications, including duplicate steering controls at the rear, all three types were produced as armoured cars. The armoured hulls in the first vehicles of the three makes differed from each other but eventually a standardised form was developed with only slight modifications (such as the bonnet length and form of radiator protection) for each chassis manufacturer.

The armoured hulls were supplied by Deutsche Edelstahl of Hanover and Deutsche Werke of Kiel and were ballistically much in advance of those of most British armoured cars of the period.

The chassis were conventional with front-mounted engine and drive transmitted to the rear bogie (all the rear wheels were dual): suspension was by means of longitudinal leaf springs. The engines were petrol units of between 65 and 70 h.p.: six-cylinder in the case of the Daimler-Benz and Magirus and four-cylinder for the Büssing.

One disadvantage of six-wheeled chassis of this kind with a relatively long wheel-base was that the underside of the body between the front and rear wheels was liable to ground when going across rough country. To counter this tendency, the Magirus models (which were the last in production) had a roller added midway between the front wheels and the leading pair of rear wheels.

Sufficient of these cars were produced to re-equip the German Army and they performed useful service in pre-war training and exercises and even in the campaigns of 1939-40. Their deficiencies in performance were well realised, however, and from about 1938 onwards they were progressively replaced by their eight-wheeled counterparts.

Panzerkampfwagen II Ausf. c

The plans for the re-equipment of the Reichswehr were based on medium tanks armed with shell-firing guns. These were expensive and took longer to produce than light tanks, however, and it was decided to build a 10-ton tank as an interim measure to supplement the 6-ton PzKpfw I models. An upward step was the 2-cm. cannon included in the armament specification and the command position was considerably improved by the addition of a third man to the crew.

Prototype vehicles to the new specification were completed by MAN, Henschel and Krupp – in 1934 – and of these the MAN version was chosen for production. The first model of this appeared in 1935 as PzKpfw II, Ausf.a1, followed in small numbers by Ausf.a2, a3 and b which had successive improvements in engine cooling and suspension. All these earlier models had a suspension system somewhat similar to that of PzKpfw I. In the next model, Ausf. c, an entirely

different form of suspension was introduced and this, together with the more powerful 6.2-litre engine (used first in Ausf. b), gave this model a far better performance than its predecessors and created the basis of the design for most of its successors.

The Ausf. c., like the earlier models, had a rear-mounted engine and transmission through driving sprockets at the front, but the suspension consisted of five medium-sized road wheels each side, each sprung independently on leaf springs.

The PzKpfw II was employed in Poland in 1939 and in France in 1940, when the Ausf. c formed an important element. Nine hundred and fifty-five PzKpfw IIs were in service at the beginning of the Western Campaign. They could be said in one sense to have formed the backbone of panzer troops because they represented the highest number of any one type out of the 2,500 German tanks used.

Schwerer geländegängiger gepanzerter Personenkraftwagen SdKfz 247

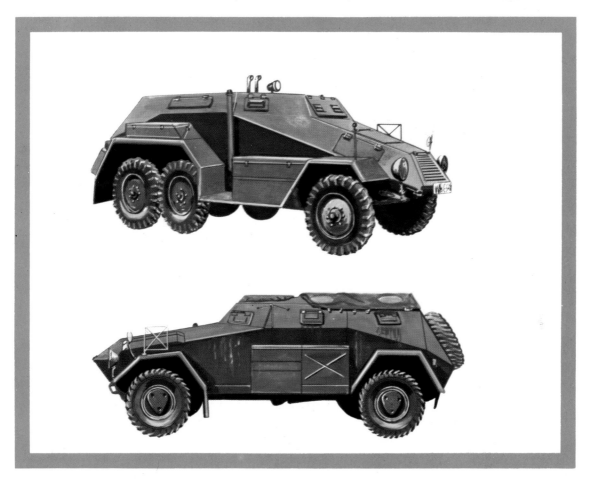

Bearing the cumbersome designation of 'heavy cross-country armoured personnel car' (sch. gl. gp. Pkw.), this type of vehicle was an armoured staff car for very senior officers and was, accordingly, produced only in very limited numbers.

The original version was built in 1937-8 on the Krupp 6×4 chassis, type L2H143, which had a four-cylinder engine of about 60 h.p. with a four-speed gearbox. About twenty were made and these were supplemented in 1939 by a similar number of vehicles built on the Horch 'standard chassis II for heavy passenger cars'. This chassis was used for a variety of unarmoured military vehicles and was similar in many respects to that used for the four-wheeled armoured cars of the SdKfz 221-223 series except that the engine was mounted at the front instead of the rear. The eight-cylinder engine was rated at about 80 h.p. and was used with a five-speed gearbox. Transmission was on all four wheels.

The armoured bodies for both six-wheeled and four-wheeled cars were similar in design and of roughly the same overall dimensions and they accommodated six men, including the driver. The armoured protection was on an 8-mm. basis.

Mittlerer Schützenpanzerwagen SdKfz 251

Germany produced both armoured and unarmoured experimental half-track vehicles in the First World War. During the rearmament phase from 1933 onwards, however, development of this type of vehicle was, at first, concentrated on the unarmoured variety for which there was a great demand for use as artillery tractors and for other purposes.

One of the advantages of a half-track is that it is possible to have a long chassis that, in a fully tracked vehicle, might be difficult to steer. At the same time, a better general performance can usually be obtained than is possible in a full-tracked vehicle of similar dimensions. It is also usually possible to use a larger quantity of standard commercial components in a half-track than could be employed in a fully tracked vehicle.

Apart from a few prototypes, all the main types of German half tracks of the Second World War had the same mechanical layout of a front engine (a six-cylinder Maybach of 100 h.p. in the case of the SdKfz 251) with transmission leading back to drive sprockets at the front of the track assembly. The front wheels were not driven and were used to support the front of

the vehicle and for steering. In a gradual turn, steering was achieved by means of the front wheels only, but further application of the steering wheel automatically brought steering brakes in the track system into operation.

The whole track assembly of the German half-tracks was complicated, expensive to produce and required a lot of maintenance, although it contributed largely to the high-speed performance of the vehicle.

The open-top armoured hull in the early versions (Ausf. A and B) of SdKfz 251 (shown in the illustrations) was assembled by means of a combination of bolting and welding.

A few 3-ton armoured personnel carriers (gepanzerter Mannschafts Transportwagen) were issued to the Army in time for the Campaign in Poland and by May 1940 they were in wide use for the Campaign in the West. Production continued throughout the War, during which some 16,000 in twenty-two different versions were built. Of these, the SdKfz 251/3 Funkwagen (Wireless vehicle) (shown in one illustration) was widely used by unit and formation commanders.

Kleiner Panzerbefehlswagen I

The need for commanders of tank units – at least up to Battalion and Regimental level – to maintain close contact with their tanks was well understood by the leaders of the German Army armoured forces, following experience gained in exercises. Gun tanks (Pzkpfw I) were at first modified as command vehicles until a more specialised command tank was developed.

The kleiner Panzerbefehlswagen ('small armoured command vehicle') was based on the chassis and running gear of the Pzkpfw I, Ausf. B. The turret was eliminated and the crew compartment was raised in height, thus providing somewhat cramped accommodation for a crew of three, two wireless sets and a map table. An observation cupola for the commander was provided in the hull roof. The only change to the automotive specification was an increase in the capacity of the dynamo, which was required in

this version to keep the wireless batteries fully charged.

One machine-gun was provided in a ball mounting in the front plate of the hull. The armour protection of the PzBefswg. was considerably increased over that of the normal gun tank version, by 17 mm. on the front plate of the crew compartment and 10 mm. on the nose plate.

The two wireless sets (models FU.2 and FU.6) enabled the unit commander on the spot to maintain contact with both sub-units and higher formation headquarters, so that effective control over the battle could be exercised. This was an important factor in the Polish Campaign when these tanks were first used. At the opening of the 1940 Campaign in the West on 10 May, ninety-six klPzBefswg. were employed – about half of the total of 200 command vehicles on PzKpfw I chassis to be built. Thirty-nine command tanks on PzKpfw II were also used at this time.

Panzerkampfwagen III Ausf. E and G

Prototypes of the 'Zugführerwagen' ('platoon commander's vehicle' – abbreviated as ZW) – the code name for the 15-ton tank – were ordered from Daimler-Benz, Rheinmetall, MAN and Krupp. These prototype vehicles were tested in 1936-7 and, as a result, the Daimler-Benz model was chosen as the basis for further development. The early models (Ausf.A, B, C and D) had varying forms of suspension (although the hull and turret were more or less standardised) ranging from five largish road wheels on coil springs per side, in the Ausf.A, to eight small wheels on leaf springs in the Ausf.B, C and D.

In the Ausf.E a more powerful Maybach twelve-cylinder engine (model HL 120 TR) was fitted – this had an output of 300 h.p., compared with the 230-250 h.p. of the earlier models. The engine was mounted at the rear of the hull and transmitted power through a hydraulic clutch and a Maybach Variorex ten-speed gearbox to the driving sprockets at the front.

The turret of the Panzer III was situated approximately in the centre of the hull and mounted the main armament of a 3.7-cm. gun. General Guderian had wanted a 5-cm. gun for the Panzer III but in order

to get production under way without controversy the smaller gun of the same calibre as the standard infantry anti-tank gun was accepted. It was not, in fact, until after the French campaign that the 5-cm. gun began to be fitted to Panzer IIIs. Coaxial armament was one machine-gun (MG 34) and another was mounted in the front of the hull beside the driver.

A few PzKpfw IIIs, mainly the earliest models, but including some Ausf.Es, were used in the Polish Campaign. In May 1940, at the beginning of the campaign in the West, 349 Panzer IIIs were employed and formed the core of the attack.

Some 3,200 tanks were available at the beginning of the campaign in Russia in June 1941 and a high proportion of these were Panzer IIIs. By this time a 5-cm. gun had been introduced into the PzKpfw III by progressive replacement of the 3.7-cm. weapon in existing vehicles.

The pictures show a PzKpfw III, Ausf.E, as it appeared (with the unusual tactical number 200) in the Western Campaign and a PzKpfw III, Ausf.G, armed with a 5-cm. KwK.L/42, of the 3rd Panzer Division in Russia.

Panzerkampfwagen IV, Ausf.A and B

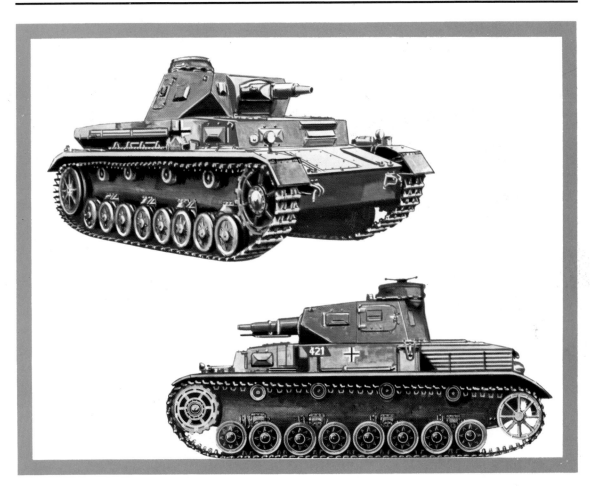

The fourth and, as it proved, the most enduring of the main types of tank with which Germany rearmed and entered the Second World War was the Panzer IV.

This was specified as a medium tank in the 20-ton class, to be armed with a 7.5-cm. gun, capable of giving fire support to the lighter tanks armed only with armour-piercing weapons or machine-guns. The code name adopted for this type was Bataillonsführerwagen (BW for short) – 'battalion commander's vehicle'.

Krupp's earlier proposals for the suspension of the BW were for interleaved road wheels of the kind that were eventually to be adopted in later tanks, but the form of suspension actually used throughout the long production run of the BW, or Panzerkampfwagen IV, as it became designated, was much more simple. The eight road wheels each side were suspended in pairs on leaf springs; the idler wheel was off the ground at the rear and the top run of the track was carried on four return rollers – an easy-to-remember recognition point for the Panzer IV. As with the other main German tanks of the period, the engine was situated at the rear with the transmission led forward to final drive via sprockets at the front of the track.

The engine was the same as that used in the Panzer III (from Ausf.E onwards) – the twelve-cylinder Maybach HL 108TR. The arrangement differed from the smaller tank in that the cooling air was drawn in at the right-hand side of the hull and after passing through the radiator was expelled through grilles at the left-hand side. The power was transmitted to the drive sprockets through a dry plate clutch and gearbox which, in the Ausf.A, had five forward speeds. This was increased to six in Ausf.B and subsequent models in which also the engine was the larger Maybach HL 120 TR (HL 120 TRM from Ausf.C onwards). These mechanical changes constituted the principal differences between the first two production models of this tank. The Pzkpfw IV Ausf.A and B are shown in the pictures, but all the earlier models of the Panzer IV were very much alike externally and all (until the introduction in early 1942, in the later vehicles of Ausf.F, of the long 7.5-cm. KwK L/43) had the short-barrelled 7.5-cm. KwK L/24 as main armament. There was a coaxial machine-gun in all tanks of the series and all except Ausf.B and C also had another MG.34 in the front of the hull to the right of the driver.

This light four-wheeled armoured car was the second model to be developed on the basis of the 'standard chassis I for heavy passenger cars'. This type of chassis (which, in spite of its designation, seems to have been used almost exclusively for armoured cars) was a rear-engined model with four-wheel drive and steering on all wheels.

The first type, SdKfz 221, was a two-man vehicle armed with a machine-gun only, but the second type, ordered in the Spring of 1940, had a hull slightly redesigned to give more room for the crew of three, and a larger turret equipped with a 2-cm. gun in addition to a machine-gun. The dual mount of these guns was intended to be fully available for anti-aircraft use and was a variant of the 2-cm. field mounting for which the turret was, in effect, a gun shield. The turret had no roof but to provide some protection against grenades was equipped with wire grilles, hinged at the sides.

The earlier light 4 × 4 armoured cars of the series had a 3,517-c.c. Horch V-8 engine but the SdKfz 222s used the Ausf.B chassis with the enlarged 3,823-c.c. engine and hydraulic instead of mechanical brakes. Weighing only about 4.7 tons, these armoured cars had a good performance and although production was ended in 1942, served well throughout the war from the French campaign onwards (the SdKfz 221 was used additionally in Poland). The performance was, to some extent, at the expense of armour, much of which was only on an 8-mm. basis. The frontal armour was to a maximum of 14.5-mm., but to supplement this a spaced shield was added experimentally in front of the nose plate of one car in the French campaign. This vehicle is shown in one of the illustrations, together with a standard SdKfz 222 in North African colours. The spaced shield was not adopted permanently for the light armoured cars although it was later a feature on some of the German eight-wheeled armoured cars.

Schützenpanzerwagen SdKfz 250 and 252

More or less a scaled-down version of the 3-ton SdKfz 251, the 1-ton SdKfz 250 series appeared some two years after the heavier vehicle. Development of this light armoured half-track was entrusted to the firms of Demag AG, who provided the chassis, and Büssing-NAG, who designed the body.

The chassis used was a shortened version of the Demag D.7 (used as a light artillery tractor, etc.) in which one of the overlapping road wheels was eliminated each side. A Maybach six-cylinder 100 h.p. engine of similar type to that employed in the SdKfz 251 series was used, in conjunction with a seven-speed gearbox. The SdKfz 250 had a better performance (37 m.p.h. maximum speed) than the SdKfz 251 and tended to be issued more widely.

Using the same chassis as the SdKfz 250, but with an armoured hull developed separately by Wegmann, the SdKfz 252 was intended specifically as an ammunition carrier for Sturmgeschütz units. This vehicle had a fully enclosed hull with a long sloping rear plate, which helped to distinguish it from the various vehicles of the SdKfz 250 series. Also, the maximum armour thickness was slightly greater. The

advantages of the special design of the SdKfz 252 were not great enough to justify an entirely different hull design, however, and the type was discontinued by 1941, when its function was taken over by versions of the SdKfz 250 series.

The SdKfz 252 did not normally carry mounted armament, but most of the vehicles of the SdKfz 250 series such as armoured personnel carriers or wireless/command vehicles frequently had a light machine-gun MG.34 mounted at the forward end of the crew compartment. The crew of vehicles of this type varied between two for ammunition carriers to six for armoured personnel carriers.

The SdKfz 250 first appeared in action in the French campaign in 1940, although it is possible that the armoured ammunition carrier SdKfz 252 was issued slightly earlier to the troops. About 7,500 vehicles of the SdKfz 250/252 type were built during the War in fourteen different versions, two of which are shown in the illustrations: a standard Schützenpanzerwagen SdKfz 250/1 (as it appeared in Russia in 1941) and an armoured ammunition carrier (le. gep. Mun. Transportswagen, SdKfz 252).

An armoured self-propelled gun to support infantry in the attack was called for in 1936, and the firms of Daimler-Benz and Krupp were selected to undertake the development of the chassis and armament respectively.

The chassis of the Panzerkampfwagen III, then under development by Daimler-Benz was, not surprisingly, chosen for the basis of the new assault gun and the armament was the 7.5-cm. L/24. This gun was similar to that mounted in the PzKpfw IV tank but as a low silhouette was required in the assault gun and all round traverse was not considered essential it was possible to have this gun on the smaller chassis with much heavier armour (50-mm. front; 30-mm. sides and rear) at a not greatly excessive increase in weight.

The prototypes and early production models of Stu G III were based on the contemporary PzKpfw III chassis models – Ausf. E and F. Later production versions likewise used the later Panzer III chassis and so,

throughout, the assault gun was mechanically the same as the tank.

The 7.5-cm. gun fitted low in the hull front plate had a traverse of 12½ degrees either side, elevation of 20 degrees and depression of 10 degrees. The short barrelled version (L/24) of the gun was fitted throughout 1940-1 and it was only in 1942 that a longer weapon began to be used.

The Stu G III was first used in small numbers in the Western Campaign in 1940, although a total of 184 was produced by the end of the year and a further 548 in 1941. Over 10,500 Stu G III of various types were completed by the end of the war.

This type of vehicle was first introduced into action by Germany and was a very successful weapon. Although later in the war production difficulties caused the Germans to use some Sturmgeschütz in place of tanks, when properly employed they were very effective.

After the design of the basic Pzkpfw II had been stabilised and production was in progress it was decided to produce also a faster version ('Schnellkampfwagen'), considered more suitable for issue to light mechanised cavalry divisions.

Daimler-Benz were asked to draw up a design for this model in which the upper hull and turret of the standard type was to be retained but in which a revised form of suspension was required in order to give the higher speeds needed. The design was undertaken in 1938 and by the following year 250 tanks were produced. The suspension used by Daimler-Benz consisted of four large road wheels each side – of Christie appearance, but with torsion-bar springing. This redesign succeeded in raising the top speed of the tank by some 5 m.p.h. although the cross-country performance proved to be inferior.

The new model appeared in two forms, PzKpfw II,

Ausf.D and E, between which the chief external difference lay in the design of the front sprocket.

The need for this fast version of the Panzer II was not sustained, however, and in 1940 it was decided to convert some of these tanks (about 100) into flamethrower vehicles. (The balance of PzKpfw II Ds and Es were subsequently converted to S.P. guns.) The conversion into flamethrowers was carried out by Wegmann of Kassell. There were minor variations in the work done, but essentially it consisted of the addition of two flame projectors – one on each front track guard – and the substitution of a smaller turret (mounting one machine-gun) for the standard turret. The flame fuel carried was sufficient for eighty bursts of 2-3 seconds from the pump-operated projectors. The range was only about 40 yards. The crew consisted of two men.

Panzerkampfwagen III Ausf.L and Ausf.M

Production of the PzKpfw III, the first models of which were built in 1937, was not finally ceased until the summer of 1943, when it was still an important element in the German armoured forces. Successive increases in armament, from the 3.7-cm. gun of the early models, through the 5-cm. L/42 of 1940 to the long 5-cm. L/60 of the late models, Ausf.L and M, associated with increased armour protection, justified the retention of ' the PzKpfw III. Even when superseded as a tank, the Panzer III chassis remained in production as the basis of assault guns.

Among the features shared by the Ausf.L and M with earlier models of the PzKpfw III were the transverse torsion-bar suspension system and the twelve-cylinder Maybach engine of 300 h.p. and the secondary armament of one machine-gun coaxial with the gun in the turret and one machine-gun in the right side of the hull, beside the driver. The maximum armour

protection of the Ausf.L and M was 70-mm. in spaced armour at the front and the combination of the increased armour and heavier gun made it necessary to reinforce the suspension. Skirt armour on hull sides and turret was also carried on some tanks. The Ausf.L and M were almost identical in appearance but in the latter, to simplify production, some vision ports and the hull escape doors were eliminated – with the introduction of skirt armour, these were, in any case, of little use.

The final version of PzKpfw III, the Ausf.N was the same as the Ausf.L or M but with the short-barrelled 7.5-cm. KwK L/24. In all, 5,644 PzKpfw IIIs were produced between 1937 and 1943.

The upper illustration shows a PzKpfw III, Ausf.M, and the lower one a PzKpfw III, Ausf.L, in winter camouflage in Russia, with the guns sheathed as protection from the cold.

Panzerkampfwagen IV Ausf.H

The Panzerkampfwagen IV, which originally entered production on a limited scale in 1937, was steadily improved in armament and armour during World War II so that it remained in production right to the end of the war, by which time about 9,000 of them had been completed. The fact that, latterly, production was continued mainly because of the urgent need for serviceable tanks in large numbers, rather than changing completely to a more modern design, is no reflection on the excellent basic design of the PzKpfw IV.

A medium tank originally specified in the 20-ton class, although in its final form at around 25 tons, the Panzer IV was powered by a 300 b.h.p. twelve-cylinder Maybach at the rear with the gearbox and final drive sprockets at the front. The suspension consisted of eight road wheels each side, suspended in pairs on leaf springs.

When the Ausf.H appeared in 1943, the main armament was the long-barrelled 7.5-cm. L/48, increasingly powerful guns having been introduced in successive models, starting with the low-velocity

7.5-cm. L/24 of the early Panzer IVs. The secondary armament remained as two machine-guns – one in the hull front and one in the turret, coaxial with the 7.5-cm. gun. The maximum armour protection was 80-mm., having been increased four-fold over that of the original version, Ausf.A. Skirting plates (or wire mesh, in some cases) were often added to the turret and hull sides to give protection against hollow charge projectiles.

The Ausf.J, which followed, the final version of PzKpfw IV, was very similar externally to the preceding model but incorporated detail changes. One of the most important (and a retrograde step) was the deletion of the turret power traverse, leaving only a 2-speed hand traverse system, in order to make room for increased fuel capacity (680 litres, compared with 470 for Ausf.H) to give the extra range called for by 1944.

One of the illustrations shows a tank partly painted with 'Zimmerit', an anti-magnetic paste to repel sticky bombs; both tanks shown have both hull and turret skirting plates.

The Panther, together with the Russian T-34 which was the direct cause of its inception, was one of the best tanks of World War II and one which has had much influence on post-war tank design.

Once the full effect of the T-34 was appreciated, it was at first proposed that a close copy should be built in Germany to counter it, but this was soon proved to be impracticable because of the fresh tooling that would have been required and the absence of suitable raw materials. The main features of the T.34 were, however, reproduced in the two designs submitted, ranging from the Daimler-Benz VK 3002, which was closely similar to the T.34, to the MAN version, which had more traditional German features. In spite of Hitler's preference for the Daimler-Benz design, the MAN model was chosen for production, which commenced in November 1942.

The Panther, as the PzKpfw V was named, had the long sloping glacis plate of the T.34, inward sloping hull sides above track level, a turret mounting a long 7.5-cm. gun (L/70-70 calibres long) and interleaved road wheels, sprung on transverse torsion bars. Armour protection was at a maximum of 120-mm. on the

turret and 80-mm. on the hull. A Maybach twelve-cylinder engine developing 642 b.h.p. (increased to 690 b.h.p. in the later models, Ausf.A and G) gave a top speed of about 28 m.p.h.

The Ausf.D was followed in production by the illogically designated Ausf.A which incorporated various improvements, one of the most obvious of which was the replacement of the unusual vertical-letter box type of mounting for the hull machine-gun by a more conventional ball-mounting. The turret was equipped with a new type of cupola and the pistol ports and loading door, present in the Ausf.D, were eliminated.

The final model of Panther, Ausf.G, had further changes, partly to compensate for shortages of raw materials and to simplify production. The driver's vision port was replaced by a rotating periscope, leaving the glacis plate clear except for the machine-gun ball mount; the hull sides were more sloped and stowage boxes at the rear were included inside the armour.

The illustrations show a Panther Ausf.D (bottom view) and an Ausf.G.

Tiger I Panzerkampfwagen

Perhaps the tank which created the greatest impression on British troops in World War II, from the time it was first encountered by them in Tunisia in 1943, was the Tiger. First used in action in September 1942 in Russia, the Tiger's design was completed before features exemplified by the Russian T.34 could be incorporated. Nevertheless, the heavy armour (at a maximum of 110-mm. on the turret and 100-mm. on the hull) and the powerful 8.8-cm. gun (KwK 36 L/55) made the Tiger a very formidable tank right to the end of the war.

Work on various heavy tank projects was started as early as 1937. These were modified with changing requirements and with the incorporation of an 8.8-cm. gun resulted in 1942 in the specification V.K. 4501, for

which the design competition was won by Henschel.

In spite of its size, the Tiger was fairly conventional in layout and design except that interleaved road wheels in the suspension system were used for the first time in a production tank although they were, of course, already a familiar feature in German half-tracks.

The engine – at the rear, the transmission being led forward via an 8-speed gearbox to front drive sprockets – was a V-form twelve-cylinder Maybach of 650 b.h.p., increased to 700 b.h.p. in the later vehicles to be built. This produced a top speed of 24 m.p.h., quite satisfactory for a 54-ton tank.

A total of 1,350 Tiger Is was manufactured and they were used in action in North Africa, Sicily, Italy, North West Europe and Russia.

Tiger II Panzerkampfwagen VI

Known to the Western Allies as King Tiger or Royal Tiger, the Tiger II or Tiger Ausf.B was even more feared by its opponents than Tiger I. With an even more powerful gun (8.8-cm., 71 calibres long, compared with Tiger I's 56 calibres) thicker armour and a sloping hull glacis plate, the Tiger II had all the best features of its predecessor, together with improvements suggested by experience in Russia. Development of the type was called for in the autumn of 1942 and when the Tiger IIs were delivered to the troops in 1944 they were the most powerful tanks in service in the world, as well as the heaviest, and the position remained unchanged until nearly the end of the War.

Fortunately for its opponents, the Tiger II was mechanically unreliable, a fault perhaps due to insufficient time being allowed for development. Fourteen tons heavier than Tiger I, the King Tiger had a similar mechanical layout but the road wheels, sprung on independent torsion bars, were not interleaved, as in Tiger I, although they were overlapped. Four hundred and eighty-five Tiger IIs were built, of which the first fifty had different, more rounded, turrets than had been built for a Porsche-designed Tiger II, although the Porsche tank itself was rejected.

The relatively few Tiger IIs built were used in 1944-45 with considerable effect on both Germany's East and West fronts.

The Jagdpanzer 38(t) Hetzer ('Baiter') was one of the best self-propelled mountings for its size of World War II, being compact, well-armoured and mobile, with a top speed of about 25 m.p.h. The gun – the 7.5-cm. Pak 39 (L/48) was mounted on the right-hand side of the sloping glacis plate, which was armoured to a maximum of 60-mm. The driver sat at the left, the 150 b.h.p. six-cylinder Praga engine being at the rear. The suspension was of the leaf spring variety, the large road wheels being sprung in pairs.

An interesting feature of the Jagdpanzer 38(t) was the type of machine-gun mounted on the roof in some vehicles. This was fitted with a deflection device which enabled it to 'fire round corners', thus making it more effective in close-up defence.

The last type on the Czech LT-38 chassis to go into production, 1,577 Hetzers were built in 1944 and the design was considered good enough to be adopted by the Swiss Army in the post-war years.

StuH Sturmgeschütz III/10.5-cm

The Sturmgeschütz III was one of Germany's most enduring armoured fighting vehicles, production of which commenced in 1940 and continued right through to the end of the war, when over 10,500 vehicles had been built.

In its standard form the StuG III was originally equipped with the low-velocity 7.5-cm. L/24 gun, suitable for close support of infantry. This was replaced in 1942 by the much more powerful L/43 and L/48 weapons which were also capable of tackling tanks. Also developed in 1943 was a new version for the close support role, but with a much heavier gun – the 10.5-cm. howitzer. The first vehicles had the 1eFH18 (light field howitzer) but the StuH.42 (assault howitzer) was soon standardized for the majority of 10.5-cm. StuG.III that were produced.

The chassis of the StuG III remained throughout production that of the contemporary model of Pzkpfw III, although the tank itself was eventually withdrawn from production in favour of the assault gun. The armour protection in the later StuG III was at a maximum of 80 mm. and side skirting plates were usually fitted. The total weight was nearly 24 tons, although the maximum speed of 24 m.p.h. remained the same as in earlier models.

The upper illustration shows a vehicle with 'Zimmerit' finish and skirting plates.

Panther-Jagdpanther 8.8-cm. Panzerjäger

Like the tank on which it was based, the Jagdpanther was a formidable vehicle. Following the standard German practice of using a tank chassis to mount a heavier gun in a limited traverse mounting, thus keeping the weight within reasonable bounds, the Panther chassis was used to create a highly mobile heavily armed 'tank hunter'.

The running gear and lower chassis of the Panther (Ausf.G) was retained but the hull was increased in height and the gun – the 8.8-cm. L/71 (71 calibres long) – was mounted in the centre of the sloping glacis plate. A ball-mounted machine-gun was retained but higher up the glacis than in the tank.

Produced in 1944 the Jagdpanther was considered by some at the time to be an undesirable dilution of Panther production, but in the defensive operations of 1944-45, the Jagdpanther was probably an even more effective weapon than the tank.

Elefant Jagdpanzer Tiger (P)

Dr Ferdinand Porsche's design to the V.K. 4501 specification – the Tiger tank – had interesting and unusual features, such as petrol-electric drive and longitudinal torsion-bar suspension, but the more conventional Henschel design was chosen for the production order for the Tiger. Nevertheless, a limited order for ninety Porsche Tiger chassis was awarded. Five were completed at the Nibelungenwerke in Austria as tanks (and used for trials only) and the rest were modified at the Alkett concern in Berlin as 'tank hunters'. This involved the addition of a fixed superstructure (armoured to a maximum of 200-mm.) in which an 8.8-cm. Pak L/71 was mounted, with a limited traverse. The original engine intended by Porsche was replaced by two twelve-cylinder Maybach engines, totalling 640 b.h.p. but the electric transmission was retained. Weighing 67 tons, the top speed was only 12½ m.p.h.

Named at first Ferdinand (after Dr Porsche) and later Elefant, these Jagdpanzers were employed at first in Russia and later, in reduced numbers, in Italy. Experience in Russia showed that the lack of a hull machine-gun was a serious fault, and one was incorporated later.

Marder III 7.5-cm. Pak auf Gw. 38(t) Ausf.M

The Czech LT-38 tank was continued in production after the German take-over of Czechoslovakia. By 1942, the Pzkpfw 38(t), as it was then called, was outclassed as a battle tank, but it was thought well worthwhile to continue output of the reliable, sturdy and easily maintained chassis as a mounting for self-propelled weapons.

The earlier self-propelled mountings (Geschützwagen – Gw.) used the chassis with the original layout in which the engine was located at the rear. The later versions, built in 1943-44, had the engine (a six-cylinder 150 b.h.p. Praga) moved forward to a position alongside the driver, and were designated Ausf.M (M = mitte [middle]), the earlier version being Ausf.H = heckmotor [rear engine]). Apart from better weight distribution, a lower silhouette was possible with the engine relocated and there were advantages in the crew having access to the gun from the rear.

The weapon used was the 7.5-cm. Pak 40/3, of a calibre length of 46, and mounted behind a shield open at the rear and with no overhead protection. One machine-gun was usually carried for local defence.

Seven hundred and ninety-nine Marder III, Ausf.M were built in 1943-44, together with four hundred and eighteen of the earlier Ausf.H in 1942-43.

Two views of different vehicles are shown above.

Wirbelwind Flakpanzer IV (3.7-cm.) Möbelwagen and Flakpanzer IV (2-cm.)

The overwhelming Allied air superiority by 1943 made it increasingly necessary for Germany to direct a greater proportion of armoured fighting vehicle production to the output of anti-aircraft tanks.

The Pzkpfw IV chassis was used for some of the more important of the A.A. tank designs which entered service in 1943-44. The commonest of the lighter weapons were the quadruple 20-mm. and the single 3.7-cm. guns. The earlier design for both of these mountings (called Möbelwagen – furniture van – in the case of the 3.7-cm. mounting) consisted of the guns with their normal shield, surrounded by a hinged four-sided square armoured structure, which folded flat, when required, to give unimpeded all-round traverse.

The later design, again generally similar for both 20-mm. and 3.7-cm. guns called Wirbelwind (Whirlwind) for the former and Ostwind (East Wind) for the latter, dispensed with the clumsy folding shields and used instead a multi-sided pot-shaped turret, open at the top. Although only lightly armoured (16-mm.) this turret gave better protection to the gun crew.

In addition to the anti-aircraft weapon, Wirbelwind and Ostwind (unlike the Möbelwagen types) retained the front hull machine-gun of the standard Pzkpfw IV.

Schwerer Ladungsträger (Sdkfz 301) and Leichter Ladungsträger (SdKfz 302)

These two machines, heavy and light demolition vehicles, were more commonly known as B.IV and Goliath, respectively. The B.IV, designed by the Borgward company of Bremen and produced from 1942 onwards, carried a 500 kg. explosive charge in a wedge-shaped bin at the front. With a seat for one man, the B.IV could be driven close to the scene of the action. In the attack, the vehicle was radio controlled. At the target, the bolts holding the demolition charge were destroyed by an electrically detonated charge, allowing the explosive bin to slide to the ground. The vehicle was then reversed away before the demolition charge was detonated. Powered by a petrol engine, the B.IV could be controlled by radio up to distances of about 1¼ miles. The first model, Ausf.A, shown in the illustration, weighed 3.6 tons. A total of 1,193 B.IV's (in three models) was produced between 1942 and 1944. They were used chiefly by heavy tank units to help destroy fixed defences.

The lighter demolition vehicle SdKfz 302 or 'Goliath' was, unlike the B.IV, expendable. About 5 ft 4 in. long, the Goliath (Ausf.A) carried a 60 kg. explosive charge. Driven by one electrical starter motor for each track, the vehicle was guided, and detonated when it reached its target, through a 3-core electric cable, of which about 670 yards was carried on a drum at the rear. In front of the drum was a compartment containing the control gear and the explosive was in a third compartment. Some 2,650 Goliaths of this type were built between 1942 and 1944 together with 5,079 (between 1943 and 1945) of a later and slightly heavier model, Ausf.B or SdKfz 303, powered by a Zündapp petrol engine. The employment of Goliaths was similar to that of the B.IV.

In the illustration of a Goliath (Ausf.A) the cover over the rear compartment is shown raised, revealing the electric control cable reel.

Leichter Schützenpanzerwagen SdKfz 250/8 and Leichter Schützenpanzerwagen SdKfz 250/9

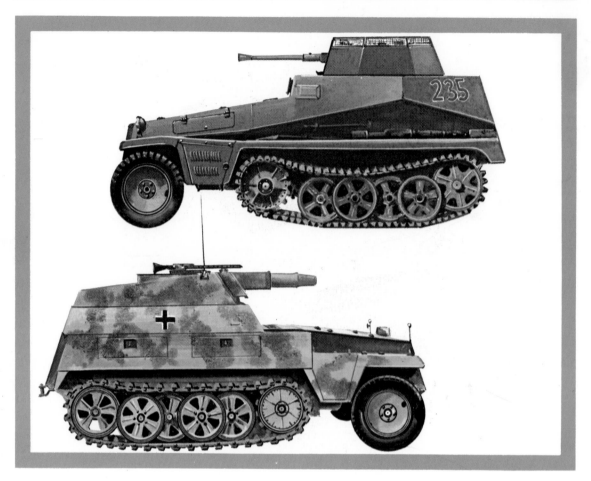

The light armoured semi-tracked armoured personnel carrier SdKfz 250 which first appeared in action as a troop carrier in 1940, had by the end of the war appeared in twelve main variants, many of which were support vehicles for the basic infantry carrier.

The SdKfz 250/8 was a self-propelled mounting for the 7.5-cm. KwK L/24 – the gun used in the earliest versions of the Sturmgeschütz III although in a 6-ton vehicle only light protection could be afforded. The gun was mounted just behind the driver together with a machine-gun (MG 42) both for ranging the 7.5-cm. KwK and for general targets.

Virtually a semi-tracked light armoured car (Panzerspähwagen) the SdKfz 250/9 had the same turret as the Leichter Panzerspähwagen SdKfz 222. This turret carried a 2-cm. gun and machine-gun on a mounting also capable of anti-aircraft fire: the only overhead protection was a hinged wire mesh frame to guard against grenades.

With good mobility and a high top speed of nearly 40 m.p.h., the SdKfz 250 series were powered by a Maybach six-cylinder engine of 100 b.h.p., which drove the tracks via front drive sprockets. The front wheels were for steering only and were not driven. An efficient vehicle, although with a somewhat complicated suspension and track design making heavy demands on maintenance time, the SdKfz 250 and its larger counterpart the SdKfz 251 was not replaced in production by semi-tracks of simpler design until 1944.

Panzerspähwagen SdKfz 234/2 (Puma) and Panzerspähwagen SdKfz 234/3

An improved version of the successful German eight-wheeled armoured car, first issued in 1938, appeared in 1944. Although the chassis was basically unaltered and only minor changes were made to the armoured hull, the use of a diesel engine of greatly increased power (the Czechoslovakian Tatra twelve-cylinder V-form of 220 b.h.p.) led to improved performance. An air-cooled diesel engine was specified in 1940, when the design work began, with the object of facilitating operation in hot countries but this type of engine was also an advantage in subsequent operations in the cold weather in Russia and the fuel economy of the diesel resulted in a much wider range.

The first model of the new eight-wheeled armoured car, SdKfz 234/1, was armed only with a 2-cm. KwK and

one machine-gun in an open-topped turret – no more than that of the 5 ton light armoured car SdKfz 222, and very inadequate for a vehicle of this size. The next model, SdKfz 234/2, was equipped with a 5-cm. (L/60) gun and a machine-gun in an enclosed turret, which made it capable of engaging tanks, although it was still intended only as a reconnaissance vehicle.

Two further models of the SdKfz 234 were produced as self-propelled mountings with guns mounted to fire forwards, with only limited traverse. The SdKfz 234/4 was a highly mobile 'tank hunter' with a 7.5-cm. Pak L/48 and the SdKfz 234/3 – shown in one of the illustrations, together with SdKfz 234/2 – was a close support vehicle with the low velocity 7.5-cm. Stu.K L/24.

Backbone of the German divisional artillery was this 105-mm. light field howitzer Model 18. The inset drawing shows a typical single-canister smoke shell used for producing smoke screens or, with coloured smoke, for signalling.

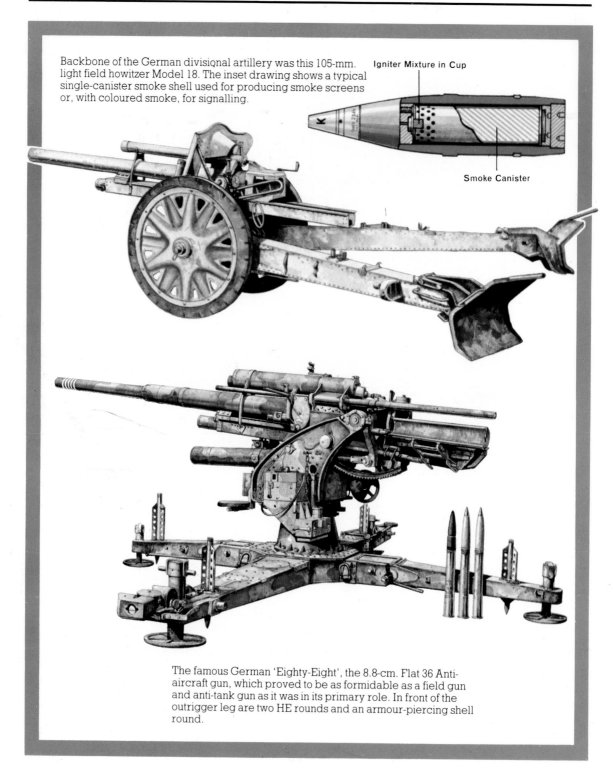

Igniter Mixture in Cup

Smoke Canister

The famous German 'Eighty-Eight', the 8.8-cm. Flat 36 Anti-aircraft gun, which proved to be as formidable as a field gun and anti-tank gun as it was in its primary role. In front of the outrigger leg are two HE rounds and an armour-piercing shell round.

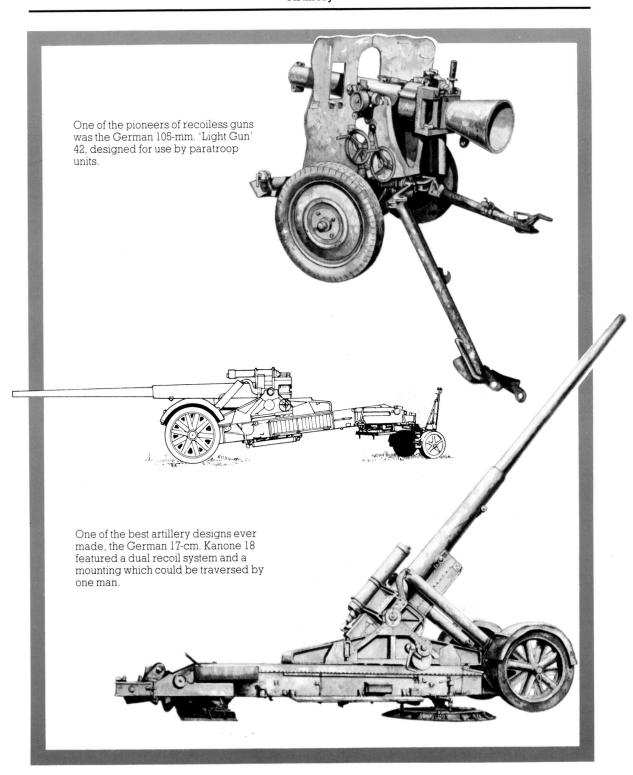

One of the pioneers of recoiless guns was the German 105-mm. 'Light Gun' 42, designed for use by paratroop units.

One of the best artillery designs ever made, the German 17-cm. Kanone 18 featured a dual recoil system and a mounting which could be traversed by one man.

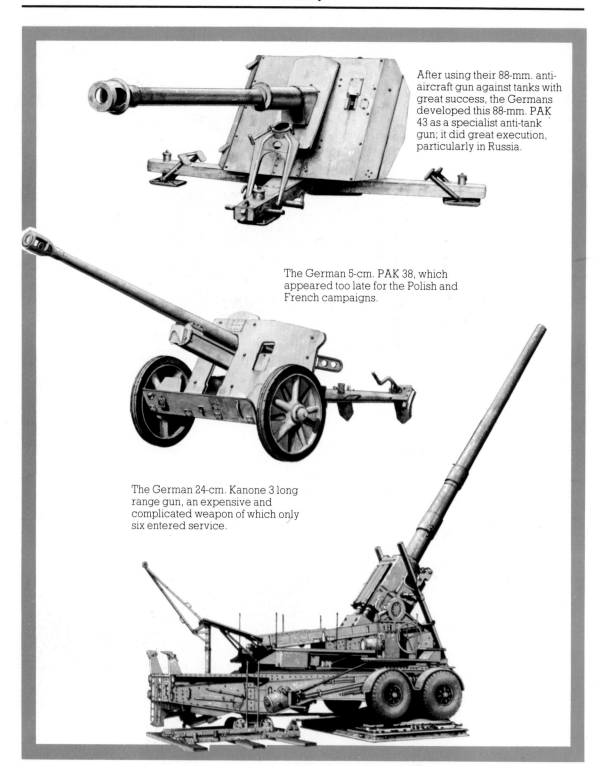

After using their 88-mm. anti-aircraft gun against tanks with great success, the Germans developed this 88-mm. PAK 43 as a specialist anti-tank gun; it did great execution, particularly in Russia.

The German 5-cm. PAK 38, which appeared too late for the Polish and French campaigns.

The German 24-cm. Kanone 3 long range gun, an expensive and complicated weapon of which only six entered service.

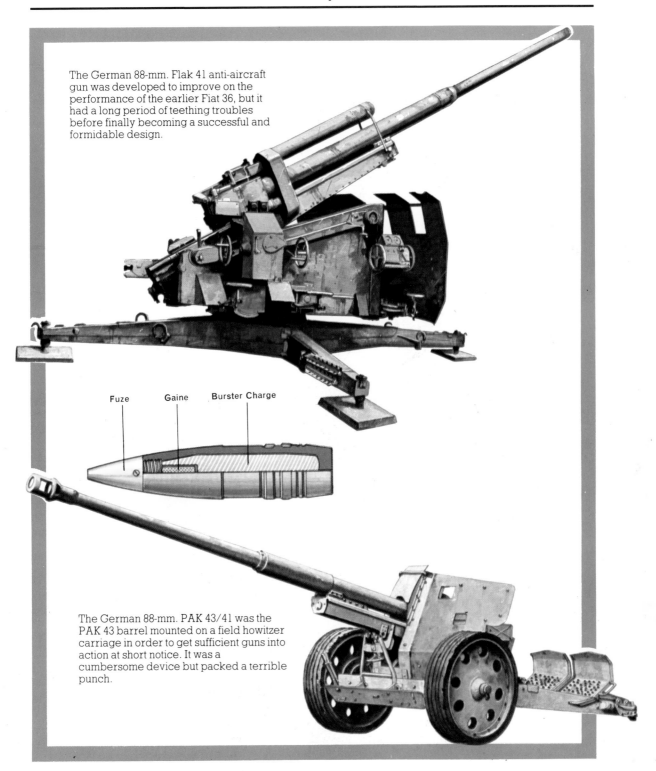

The German 88-mm. Flak 41 anti-aircraft gun was developed to improve on the performance of the earlier Fiat 36, but it had a long period of teething troubles before finally becoming a successful and formidable design.

Fuze   Gaine   Burster Charge

The German 88-mm. PAK 43/41 was the PAK 43 barrel mounted on a field howitzer carriage in order to get sufficient guns into action at short notice. It was a cumbersome device but packed a terrible punch.

Carro Armato L.3/35

Yet another member of the family of the Carden-Loyd Mark VI, which, by direct sales and the granting of manufacturing licences, spread to many of the countries of the world in the 1930s, was this small Italian tank.

Twenty-five Carden-Loyd Mark VIs were purchased by the Italian Army in 1929 and, based on these, a model known as Carro Veloce ('fast tank') C.V.28 was built by the Fiat motor works in conjunction with the Ansaldo armaments concern. This was followed by further models, C.V.29 and C.V. L.3/33. The Carro Veloce L.3/35 was the final model and included some improvements over the L.3/33, although up-dated examples of the earlier model existed and so the differences between the two are often small.

The L3/35's engine was a four-cylinder Fiat of 43 h.p., mounted transversely at the rear with the radiator – a circular type with centrifugal fan – behind it. The transmission was led forward to the clutch and gearbox

(with four forward speeds) in front of the driver, with final drive to front track sprockets. The suspension consisted of two three-wheel bogie units and a single, unsprung, road wheel (just in front of the rear idler wheel) each side. Each bogie unit was sprung on a quarter-elliptic leaf spring.

The fighting compartment of the L.3/35 was in the centre of the vehicle with the two crew members – driver on the right and gunner on the left – sitting side by side. The armoured superstructure varied in that in the earlier tanks built it was constructed of plates riveted on to angle girders whereas in later vehicles bolts were employed. Maximum armour thickness was 13.5 mm. The standard armament was two 8-mm. Breda model 38 machine-guns with a total traverse of 24 degrees, elevation of 15 degrees and depression of 12 degrees. There was also a flamethrower version in which the flame projector replaced one of the machine-guns.

Some interesting mechanical features were included in this armoured car, the prototype of which, built by Spa, was completed by mid-1939. The most unusual point about the Autoblinda 40 was its transmission system. From the rear-mounted engine (a six-cylinder Spa of 80 h.p.) the drive was transmitted through a dry plate clutch to a five-speed and overdrive crash-type gearbox, built integrally with the clutch housing. All speeds except the fifth and overdrive sixth were also available in reverse. From the gearbox the drive was transmitted to a distribution box located approximately in the centre of the vehicle and incorporating a differential unit. The drive direct to each wheel was taken by helical bevel gear wheels through universally jointed shafts: a layout in plan which resembled a St. Andrew's cross.

The steering system operated on all four wheels and for emergency driving in reverse a second steering wheel, together with basic driving controls, was fitted.

The suspension was of the independent coil spring type and the brakes hydraulic.

The hull of the AB 40 consisted of flat armour plates, varying between 8½-mm. and 6-mm. bolted or riveted to a framework, the whole being bolted to the chassis frame. The turret (armoured to a maximum of 18-mm. and minimum of 6-mm.) was derived from an early design for the L.6/40 tank and mounted two 8-mm. Breda machine-guns. The fixed armament was completed by a further 8-mm. machine-gun mounted at the rear of the fighting compartment, at the right-hand side, to fire over the engine.

Two drivers, a commander/gunner and a rear gunner made up the crew of the AB 40. Weighing about 6½ tons and with a top speed of 46 m.p.h., the AB 40 was a suitable reconnaissance vehicle for employment in the North African desert and this was where it was mainly used, although its successor the AB 41 also saw service in Russia.

Carro Armato L. 6/40

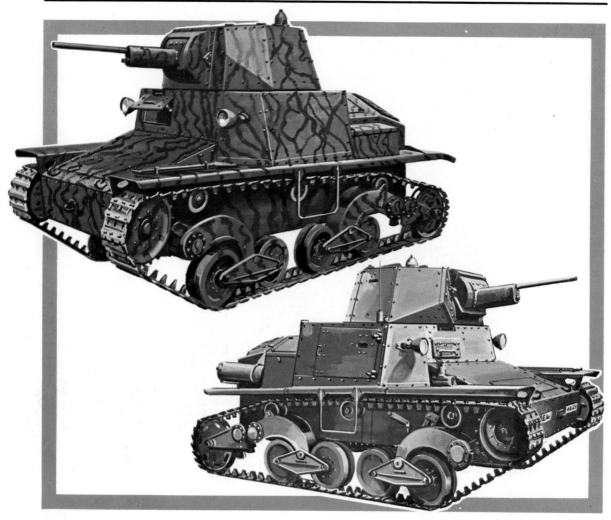

Fiat designed a light tank in 1936 to replace the L.3 series, and after several changes were made, principally to the suspension and the armament, the design emerged as the L.6/40 which was issued to the Italian Army in 1940-1. The L.6/40 was more or less a scaled-up L.3 with a more powerful engine (a four-cylinder Spa of 70 h.p.) and torsion-bar suspension and equipped with a turret.

With armour to a maximum of 30-mm. and armed with a 20-mm. gun and coaxial 8-mm. machine-gun, the

L.6/40 was a considerable improvement on its predecessor. However, with a crew of only two men and still too lightly armed, the tank was not a great success in combat. It was used in action in North Africa from about 1941 onwards and, later, in Russia as a reconnaissance vehicle.

The illustrations both show L.6/40s in European colour schemes; one in the plain greenish-grey used in 1940-1 and the other in a camouflage pattern believed to have been used earlier in the War.

Retaining the main mechanical features of the M.11/39, the Carro Armato M.13/40 was a great improvement as a fighting vehicle in that the main gun was both much more powerful and was mounted in a fully rotating turret.

The prototype of this 13-ton medium tank appeared early in 1940 and, because of the likelihood of Italy soon entering the War, production was hurried on so that the first production vehicles were ready by July of the same year.

A factor which must have greatly simplified the production of the M.13/40 was that the lower hull was almost identical to that of the M.11/39, although the Spa 8T diesel engine was improved to give 125 h.p. The opportunity was taken at the same time of redesigning some features of the steering and final drive system to make for a more compact and efficient layout. Also, in order to carry the greater weight of the M.13/40, the suspension was strengthened and an extra leaf was added to the semi-elliptic springs.

The main armament consisted of an Ansaldo-built 47-mm. gun, 32 calibres long, mounted coaxially with an 8-mm. Breda model 38 machine-gun in a hydraulically traversed turret. In addition to this, two Breda 38 machine-guns were in a twin mounting in the front right-hand side of the hull, where they had a total traverse of 30 degrees. Armour protection of the M.13/40 was on a 40-mm. basis for the turret front and 30-mm. for the hull.

First used in action in December 1940 in North Africa, the M.13/40 and its developments were the best Italian tanks to go into service in quantity in the Second World War. Although inferior to contemporary German tanks it was at least comparable in many respects to British cruiser tanks of its era and was one of the very few types of captured tank to be used in some numbers by the British forces – both Australian and United Kingdom armoured regiments used them in Libya in 1941.

The illustrations show the 5th tank, 1st platoon, in the 1st Company of an Italian tank battalion in North Africa, about 1941.

Carro Armato M.15/42

The Italian medium tank M.15/42 was a logical development of the M.13/40 of 1940 and its derivative the M.14/41. Very much like its predecessors in appearance, the M.15/42's's 47-mm. gun was, however, of 40 calibres length (compared with 32 calibres of the earlier tanks) which gave it a far higher muzzle velocity and greater penetrative power.

The other most important change compared with the M.13/40 and M.14/41 was a more powerful engine, the S.P.A. 15TB which produced 192 b.h.p. and gave a better maximum (road) speed of 25 m.p.h., despite the increase of a ton in weight. Although the new engine provided the extra power needed, it was a petrol engine and it seems to have been a backward step to abandon the diesel type previously used.

Other features of the M.15/42 were a crew of four, an armament of three 8-mm. Breda machine-guns (one coaxial, two in a dual mount in the front of the hull) besides the 47-mm. gun; and maximum armour protection of 45-mm. (50-mm. on the gun mantlet).

About 2,000 M.13/40s and M.14/41s were completed (of which about the last 800 were the latter) but production of the Carro Armato M.15/42 ceased after only 82 of them were bult by early 1943. Following this, Italian armoured fighting vehicle production was concentrated on self-propelled guns.

One illustration shows the fifth tank of the 1st Company, 2nd Platoon, of an Italian armoured battalion in Italy in 1943; the other an M.15/42 in desert colours.

Carro Armato P.40

The only Italian heavy tank of World War II, the P.40, which entered production in 1943, had it origin in design studies commenced in 1938. One of the two Ansaldo designs (in competition with two drawn up by the official Direzione della Motorizzazione) was chosen in 1940, although the first prototype to be built did not appear until early 1942.

A 26-ton vehicle, protected up to a maximum of 50-mm., a high velocity 75-mm. gun was chosen as the main armament. As the gun being developed for it was not ready when the prototype was completed, however, the 75/18 howitzer was mounted instead. This was replaced in the second prototype by the interim gun 75/32 until, with the third prototype, the 75/34, with a muzzle velocity of 610 metres per second, could be used.

The suspension of the P.40 followed the common Italian practice of two groups of four road wheels each

side carried on a semi-elliptic leaf spring for each group – a somewhat crude but well-tried system. The hull and turret layouts were conventional, the armament of the 75-mm. gun and coaxial 8-mm. machine-gun being concentrated in the turret – the front hull machine-gun which existed in the first two prototypes was eliminated in the final version.

The engine was at the rear, the transmission being led forward via the gearbox and clutch to track drive sprockets at the front. The prototypes used a 330 h.p. diesel but a new twelve-cylinder-V petrol engine of 420 h.p. was ready for use in the production models, to which it gave a maximum speed of 25 m.p.h.

Only twenty-one P.40s had been completed by the time of the Armistice in 1943. Two Italian tank battalions to be equipped with P.40s were in the process of formation at this time, but in the end only the Germans employed in service the few P.40s available.

Semovente M. 42M da 75/34 and Semovente M.42L da 105/23

Some of the most effective Italian armoured fighting vehicles were the series of assault guns based on medium tank chassis which appeared from 1941 onwards.

These vehicles were fully armoured and enclosed, and mounted weapons ranging in power from the 75/18 (75-mm.; 18 calibres long) howitzer originally used on the M.13/40 chassis, to the 105/23 on the M.15/42 chassis.

The 75/18 Semovente was in production between 1941 and 1943: later vehicles used the M.14/41 and M.15/42 chassis. In all, 780 vehicles were built. They gave good service with the Ariete and Littorio Divisions in North Africa and later on Italian soil.

The prototype for the Semovente 75/34 was completed by the end of 1942, by which time a total of 500 had been ordered. Due to problems over the design of the mounting for the 75/34, however, 75/18s or 75/32s were fitted in M.15/42 chassis intended for the new gun. In the end, only just over ninety 75/34 assault guns were built.

The Semovente M.42M da 75/34 was considered to be a good 'tank hunter', its gun having a muzzle velocity of 610 metres per second and a range of 12½ kilometres. Apart from the longer gun, it was similar in most external respects to the early 75/18 and 75/32 assault guns on the chassis of M.13/40, M.14/41 and M.15/42 tanks, all of which had similar running gear. Weighing 15 tons, the Semovente M.42M da 75/34 was powered by a S.P.A. eight-cylinder petrol engine of 192 b.h.p. which gave it a top speed of about 25 m.p.h. The vehicle had a crew of three men and an 8-mm. machine-gun was carried for anti-aircraft defence.

The Semovente M.42L da 105/23 was in general appearance like the 75-mm. assault gun but had a much larger 105-mm. 23-calibre length, howitzer, specially developed as an assault gun. The final prototype was ready in January 1943, and firing trials took place later in that month. Deliveries began in May 1943 but, although 454 of them were finally ordered, only a relatively small number was completed.

With the same 192 b.h.p. petrol engine, the Semovente 105/23 weighed somewhat more at 15.6 tons than earlier models and had a top speed of 22 m.p.h. The 105-mm. gun was a good anti-tank weapon, notably with its special ammunition.

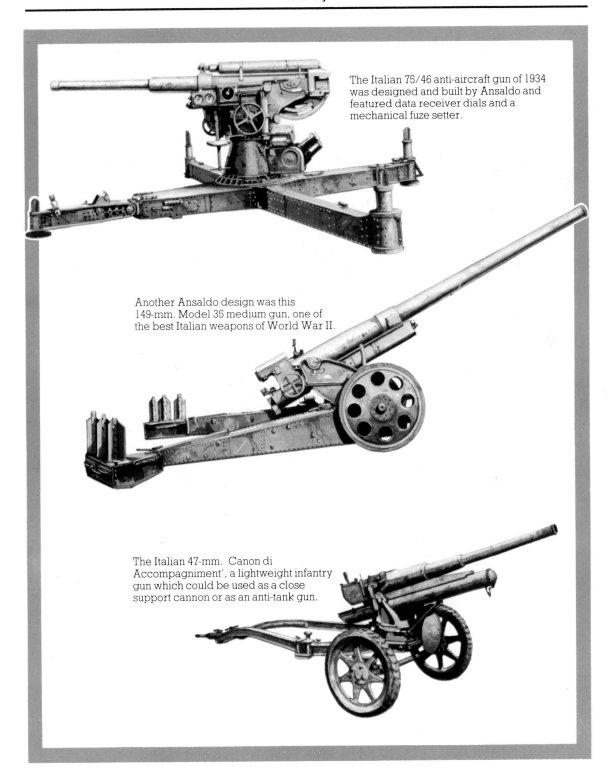

The Italian 75/46 anti-aircraft gun of 1934 was designed and built by Ansaldo and featured data receiver dials and a mechanical fuze setter.

Another Ansaldo design was this 149-mm. Model 35 medium gun, one of the best Italian weapons of World War II.

The Italian 47-mm. Canon di Accompagniment', a lightweight infantry gun which could be used as a close support cannon or as an anti-tank gun.

Bren Carrier

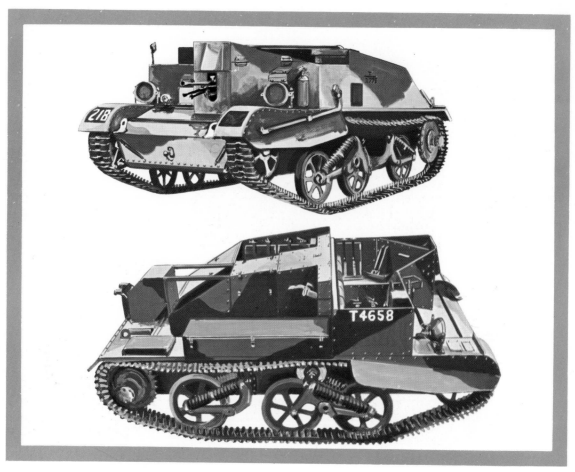

The tracked armoured carrier was one of the most characteristic vehicles of the British Army in the Second World War and around 50,000 of all types were built in the United Kingdom alone by 1945, similar vehicles being also made in quantity in Canada and the U.S.A. as well as in other Commonwealth countries.

One of the earliest types of carrier to be used in the Second World War was the Carrier, Bren, but although in this particular form, relatively few were built (then being replaced by the Carrier, Universal) the name Bren Carrier continued in popular usage for all types throughout the war.

The most interesting feature of the Bren Carrier (and all other carriers of the same mechanical design) was the steering system. This was operated by a steering wheel. When the steering wheel was turned, the front two-wheel suspension units on each side were moved laterally, being mounted on a cross-tube which ran through the vehicle. This bowed the tracks into a curve, which the vehicle followed. Further movement of the steering wheel operated track brakes on either side, causing a skid turn.

The suspension consisted, each side, of two road

wheels in one Horstmann-type bogie unit, sprung on a pair of oblique coil springs, and a single wheel unit of generally similar type. The idler wheel was at the front. Power was provided by a 65 h.p. Ford V-8 engine in the first vehicles, although later 85 h.p. Canadian or U.S.-built engines were also used.

The crew of the Carrier, Bren, consisted of three men, the driver at the right and the gunner beside him at the left with an extension of the armour in front of him to facilitate operation of the Bren gun when mounted in the vehicle (normally it was intended that the gun should be operated from the ground in normal infantry fashion). The third man sat behind the gunner in a separate compartment and the armour was extended rearwards on this side to protect him. The maximum armour thickness of the Carrier was 12-mm.

One illustration shows a Carrier, Bren, No. 2, Mark II (the No. 2 indicates a U.S.-built engine, the Mark number indicating slight changes in the hull), from above in colours used in France in 1940. The other view is of a Carrier belonging to the 2nd Battalion The Cameronians, of the 4th Indian Division in the Middle East in 1940.

Morris Reconnaissance Armoured Car (Model CS9/LAC)

Built on a modified Morris Commercial 15-cwt 4 × 2 truck chassis, this armoured car was, in effect, a stop-gap design to replace older six-wheeled armoured cars pending the development of new four-wheel-drive chassis.

After the prototype was tested in 1936, a further ninety-nine vehicles with slight modifications were ordered and these were delivered about 1938. Thirty-eight cars of this kind were taken to France by the 12th Royal Lancers, the only armoured car regiment with the British Expeditionary Force, and later, thirty were issued to the 11th Hussars in Egypt, by whom they were used in conjunction with some 1920 and 1924 pattern Rolls-Royce armoured cars, rearmed. A high performance cross-country was not expected of vehicles with conventional 4 × 2 transmission, but the 11th Hussars found that the Morris armoured cars (which were fitted with desert tyres) traversed soft sand better than the Rolls-Royce, though the springs

and steering did not stand up so well.

The Morris CS9/LAC had a six-cylinder engine of 96.2 h.p., which gave it a top speed of 45 m.p.h. The armament consisted of a 0.55-in. Boys anti-tank rifle and a 0.303-in. Bren light machine-gun mounted independently in an open-topped turret. The crew consisted of four men – commander, gunner, driver and wireless operator (who sat beside the driver).

The 12th Royal Lancers' cars did useful work in protecting the flank of the British Expeditionary Force before the evacuation from Dunkirk, when they were left behind in France.

The 11th Hussars used their Morris armoured cars in North Africa up to the Spring of 1941, although by this time some had been converted into light armoured command vehicles.

The illustration show a car ('Cowes') of C Squadron, the 12th Royal Lancers and a car of the 11th Hussars as it appeared in the Western Desert campaign.

The culmination of a long series of Light Tanks stemming from the Carden-Loyd Mark VII, designed by Sir John Carden in 1928, the Light Tanks of the Mark VI series were numerically the most important armoured fighting vehicles of the British Army in 1939-40.

Following the pattern of its predecessors the Mark VI had the engine (an 88 h.p. six-cylinder Meadows) at the right-hand side of the hull with the transmission led forward to drive front sprockets. The driver sat at the left-hand side, and the turret, containing the commander and gunner, was also off-set to the left. The suspension consisted of two two-wheeled bogie units each side, sprung on twin coil springs, the rear road wheel acting also as a trailing idler. This form of Horstmann suspension was simple and dependable.

The armament of the Mark VIB consisted of a Vickers 0.303-in. water-cooled machine-gun and a Vickers 0.5-in. heavy machine-gun. The Mark VIC, which followed the Mark VIB in production, was similar in almost all respects except that it lacked the turret cupola and had Besa machine-guns of 7.92-mm. and 15-mm. instead of the Vickers. In both models the maximum armour thickness was only 14-mm. and these tanks could be regarded as no more than reconnaissance vehicles. Nevertheless, Mark VIBs were employed in all the Divisional Cavalry Regiments of the British Expeditionary Force, and as headquarters tanks in the 1st Army Tank Brigade. Even in the 1st Armoured Division Light Mark VICs formed a high proportion of the tank strength because of the delay in delivery of Cruiser tanks and they were no match for most types of German tanks encountered in 1940.

The illustrations show a Tank, Light Mark VIB of the 4th/7th Royal Dragoon Guards (the Divisional Cavalry Regiment of the 2nd Infantry Division, B.E.F.) and a Mark VIC of the 10th Royal Hussars, one of the tank regiments of the 2nd Armoured Brigade, 1st Armoured Division.

Designed and built to the General Staff specification A.11 for a two-man infantry-accompanying tank, armoured against all known anti-tank guns and equipped with one machine-gun, the Infantry Mark I met all these requirements adequately. It also was relatively cheap to manufacture, another important consideration at the time.

Sir John Carden of Vickers-Armstrong Ltd. undertook the design, and the prototype vehicle was ready by the Autumn of 1936. A small tank, the A.11 weighed 11 tons due to its heavy armour, on a 60-mm. basis. However, as only a low speed (8 m.p.h.) was required in a tank tied closely to the infantry advance it was possible to use the readily available and inexpensive Ford V-8 lorry engine and transmission. This was sited at the rear and drove rear sprockets, much of the final drive and steering systems being closely derived from other Vickers tracked vehicles. The suspension – two four-wheeled bogie units each side, sprung on semi-elliptic springs – was similar to

that of the commercial Vickers 6-ton tank and Dragon, Medium Mark IV artillery tractor.

The armament of one Vickers 0.303-in. water-cooled machine-gun, mounted in the cast turret, was intended only for use against 'soft' targets, although the need for some means of attacking other armoured vehicles was subsequently recognised by substituting the Vickers 0.5-in. heavy machine-gun in some troop leaders' tanks.

In action, the Infantry Mark I's served their purpose quite well, within their known limitations – their armour proving to be highly effective.

The illustrations both show tanks of the 4th Battalion Royal Tank Regiment, which used an eye as its unit sign. One picture is of a tank in the 1939 plain green and the other shows a company commander's tank in France: this is one of the later production vehicles with minor changes, including the positioning of the headlamps.

Designed originally as a potential replacement for the old Medium Tanks, Marks I and II, used by the Royal Tank Corps, this tank, known originally as A.9 from its General Staff specification number, became the first of the new class of Cruiser Tanks called for under the new official policy formulated in 1936.

Sir John Carden, working for Vickers-Armstrong, designed the A.9, which followed the broad layout of the Medium Mark III (which had not been produced in numbers because of its high cost at the time) but was lighter and was intended to use a commercially available engine. An A.E.C. six-cylinder 150 h.p. engine similar to that used in buses was eventually settled on for the power unit: this was a diesel engine converted for use with petrol. The gearbox was a Meadows five-speed model.

The main armament was planned as a 3-pr (47-mm.) – the standard gun in British tanks – but this was replaced in production models by the new 2-pr

(40-mm.), which was smaller but had a higher muzzle velocity. The main turret incorporated power traverse – an innovation in British tanks at this time. In addition to the coaxial Vickers 0.303-in. machine-gun, two further Vickers guns were carried in two small auxiliary turrets – one either side of the driver's cab. A proportion of Cruiser Mark Is were fitted with a 3.7-in. howitzer instead of the 2-pr to act as close support vehicles able to put down high-explosive fire and lay smoke.

Cruiser Mark Is were used in action by the 1st Armoured Division in France in 1940 and one of the illustrations shows a close support tank of Headquarters, 'A' Squadron, 3rd Royal Tank Regiment, of this Division. They were also employed with the 2nd and 7th Armoured Division in the earlier North African campaigns and the other illustration is of a tank belonging to 1st Royal Tank Regiment of the latter formation.

The General Staff specification A.10 was for an infantry-accompanying tank. The design for this tank, produced by Sir John Carden for Vickers-Armstrong, was based very closely on that of A.9. The mechanical components of transmission and suspension were almost identical, although lower gear ratios had to be used to deal with the extra weight brought about by an increase of the armour maximum of 14-mm. on A.9 to 30-mm. (as finally specified) for A.10.

The hull design of the A.10 was simpler than that of A.9 in that the two auxiliary turrets (cramped, and highly unpopular with tank crews) were eliminated, a single machine-gun in the right-hand side of the hull, beside the driver, taking their place.

The extra armour thickness on the A.7 was achieved by bolting additional plates on to the hull and the turret. By the time the A.7 was ready for production, in early 1938, the armour maximum of 30-mm. was considered inadequate for an infantry tank (the specification for A.11 already called for 60-mm.) but it was,

nevertheless, decided to produce the A.10, although as a 'heavy cruiser' tank. Limited orders were placed with Vickers-Armstrong, Metropolitan-Cammell Carriage & Wagon Co., and Birmingham Railway Carriage & Wagon Co. for an eventual total of 160 vehicles. Most of these were completed during 1940, the last in the late autumn. Early in the course of production, the Besa 7.92-mm. machine-gun was introduced in place of the Vickers and the tanks with this weapon were designated Cruiser, Mark IIA.

One illustration shows a Cruiser Mark IIA with which the 5th Royal Tank Regiment (1st Armoured Division) was re-equipped in the United Kingdom after the withdrawal from France in 1940. This tank has no machine-guns, which were then in short supply. The other view shows a tank of the 2nd Armoured Division as it appeared in North Africa early in 1941. The addition of sand shields over the tracks and a water drum will be noticed.

The War Office was made aware in 1936 of the potential of the American Christie tank for development as a British medium or cruiser tank. With remarkable promptitude a Christie tank was purchased for the War Office (through the medium of Morris Cars Ltd, part of the Nuffield organisation) and this arrived in England in November 1936.

This tank was tested and it was decided to adopt two salient features of the design – ,a powerful Liberty modified aero engine and high-speed suspension.

A specification, A.13, was drawn up and Morris Commercial Cars Ltd, (another company of the Nuffield group) were asked to build two prototypes.

The armament on all A.13 cruiser tanks consisted of a 2-pr gun with a coaxial machine-gun in the turret. On the later Mark IVs to be produced, however, the original Vickers 0.303-in. machine-gun was replaced by a Besa 7.92-mm. and these vehicles were designated Mark IVA. A few tanks were fitted for close support with 3-in. howitzers instead of 2-prs but many

regiments re-equipped with Cruiser Mark IVs still retained earlier cruiser tanks for this function.

The engine of the Cruiser Tanks Marks III and IV was a Nuffield-built Liberty V-12 cylinder of 340 h.p. which transmitted its power via a multiplate clutch and a four-speed gearbox to rear sprockets. Steering was of the clutch and brake type. The suspension, which, with the high power/weight ratio, was mainly responsible for the A.13's good performance (30 m.p.h. maximum, reduced from the prototype's 45 m.p.h.), consisted of four large road wheels each side. These were mounted on trailing or leading pivot arms, controlled by long coil springs, contained between inner and outer walls of the hull sides.

Three hundred and thirty-five Tanks, Cruiser, Marks III, IV and IVA, were built. Some of all Marks were sent to France with the 1st Armoured Division in 1940 and others (Mark IVA) were used in action in the North African campaigns, where their speed was a great asset, until late 1941.

It can be claimed that the Infantry Mark II was one of the best British tanks of the Second World War, because at the time of its appearance on the battle scene it was at least as well armed as the majority of its German opponents and much better armoured. The counterattack by the 1st Army Tank Brigade near Arras on 21 May 1940 was the only real tactical shock received by the Germans in the invasion of France, and even Rommel (then commanding the 7th Panzer Division) described the situation at one stage as 'an extremely tight spot'. In the early Western Desert campaigns, the Matilda was superior to all Italian tanks and ruled the battlefield.

The essentials of the Infantry Mark II (later known as Matilda) were a 2-pr gun and coaxial machine-gun in the turret, armour increased to a maximum of 78-mm., a four-man crew and a top speed nearly double that of its predecessor. The general layout was the same as that of the later Vickers Medium tanks A.6 and A.7 and the suspension – two-wheeled bogie units on coil springs – was of the kind originally used in the commercial Vickers Mark C sold to Japan. To provide the necessary power and, at the same time, to ease

production problems, two standard A.E.C. diesel engines (each six-cylinder, 87 h.p.) were used in Matilda I and Matilda II, although these were replaced by Leyland diesels (total 190 h.p.) in Matilda III and subsequent models. The machine-gun coaxial with the 2-pr gun in Matilda I, the first model of Infantry Mark II, was a water-cooled Vickers 0.303-in. This was the model used with the B.E.F. in France – all were at first issued to the 7th Battalion Royal Tank Regiment although later a few were transferred to the 4th Battalion to give fire support to that unit's Infantry Mark Is. Matilda II and subsequent models used in later actions all had a Besa machine-gun replacing the Vickers.

A feature found only in the early Matildas was a higher form of suspension than that used in later production models, where the armoured skirting gave more protection to the road wheels. This early suspension is shown in both illustrations, which are of tanks of the 7th Battalion Royal Tank Regiment. Also shown in one view is the trench-crossing tail device that was designed and built hurriedly to meet a demand in march 1940 from the troops in France.

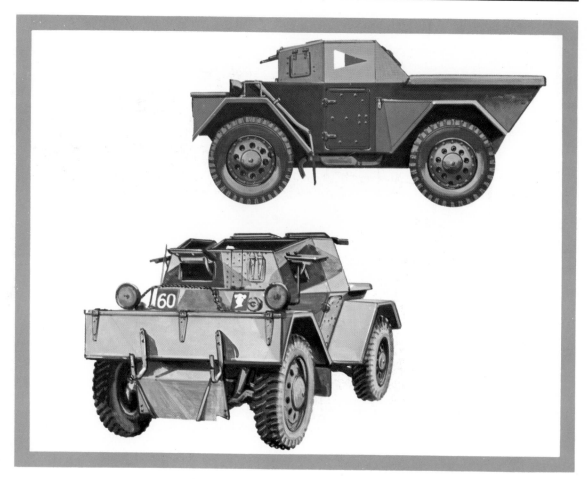

The Daimler Scout Car was one of the most effective items of equipment of its kind to be built and was widely used in the British Army for scouting and liaison purposes.

The original specification drawn up by the War Office early in 1938 called for a small vehicle with frontal armour of at least 25-mm. capable of resisting infantry light anti-tank weapons and able to head a column of tanks or other vehicles likely to encounter opposition. A 0.303-in. Bren light machine-gun was to be carried and the vehicle was to be able to withdraw quickly in reverse. For this reason only frontal armour was specified: for the sake of lightness no other armour was called for.

Three designs were submitted and tested in the latter half of 1938 and eventually the one from B.S.A. Cycles Ltd. was selected. During the development of this vehicle, light side armour was at first added, as much as a means of supporting the heavy 30-mm. glacis plate as for crew protection. Then, the War Office decided that the side armour must be to a 14-mm. standard, an armoured roof must be added and the bonnet of the engine must also be protected.

The B.S.A./Daimler (later known simply as 'Daimler') Scout Car was powered by a six-cylinder 55 h.p. engine mounted at the rear. The drive was taken forward through a 'Fluid Flywheel' and pre-selector gearbox to a transfer box in the centre of the vehicle.

The suspension was independent, using coil springs at each wheel. Steering was on all four wheels, which made for a small turning circle and, incidentally, gave considerable difficulties for drivers lacking experience. A high speed in reverse could be obtained in the Scout Car and this was facilitated for the driver by the position of his seat, which was turned inwards slightly, enabling him more readily to look over his left shoulder.

Scout Cars, Mark I, were used in action in France in 1940 with two experimental platoons of the 4th Battalion Royal Northumberland Fusiliers, an infantry division reconnaissance unit, otherwise chiefly equipped with motor-cycles. A car of this unit, with its white and red pennant is shown in one of the illustrations. The second illustration is of a Scout Car with the 2nd Armoured Division in Libya.

Valentine Infantry Tank Mark III

One of the most reliable of British tanks, the Valentine was designed as a private venture by Vickers-Armstrong Ltd and gained its name from the fact that the proposal for this new infantry tank had been deposited with the War Office just before St. Valentine's Day, 1938.

The Valentine was based on the A.9 and A.10 tanks designed by Sir John Carden, who was killed in an aeroplane accident in December 1935. The 30-mm. armour of A.10 was by 1937 no longer considered adequate for an infantry support tank and was rejected for this role, although subsequently the A.10 did enjoy limited production as a heavy cruiser tank. The Valentine, therefore, started with a 65-mm. armour basis (slightly greater than that of Infantry Tank Mark I) but took other features from the A.9 and A.10, including a similar A.E.C. six-cylinder petrol engine and transmission and the same form of suspension. Both hull and turret were more compact, though, and this limited the crew to three men only.

May 1940 was stipulated as the delivery date for the first Vickers-built Valentine and this target was achieved. When the first production vehicle was tested

by the War Office it was found to be generally satisfactory, although the engine cooling needed some improvements and the tracks were unreliable.

Output of Valentines rose steadily, while Vickers' engineers corrected their relatively simple faults, so that by mid-1941 they were being delivered at the rate of forty-five per month. The Valentine was eventually developed through eleven different Marks, although the main types in use in 1940-1 were the Valentine II (Tank, Infantry, Mark III*), in which the petrol engine was replaced by an A.E.C. six-cylinder diesel. The desire for a three-man turret was then met with in the Valentine III. All the earlier Valentines had armament of a 2-pr gun and coaxial 7.92-mm. Besa machine-gun.

Home Defence was necessarily the main role of the Valentine in 1940-1, but some were sent out to North Africa at the end of 1941. The 8th Royal Tank Regiment was equipped with Valentines at this time and a Valentine II of this unit in desert colours is shown in one of the illustrations. Another Valentine II is shown in the other view, as it appeared with the 1st Royal Gloucestershire Hussars (6th Armoured Division) on a United Kingdom training exercise in October 1941.

Standard Light Reconnaissance Cars, 4 × 2, Marks I and II (Beaverette I and II)

Most numerous of the many varieties of improvised armoured vehicles built for the defence of the United Kingdom in the emergency after the withdrawal of the British Expeditionary Force from France, the Beaverette was produced in the first instance principally for the defence of aircraft factories. The name was derived from that of Lord Beaverbrook, then Minister of Aircraft Production.

The large quantities of armour plate required could not be spared for these cars and so protection was made up from ⅜-in. or 7/16 in. mild-steel plates, with 3-in. oak planks for backing at the front of the vehicle. There was no armour at the rear and no roof. The chassis used was that of the 14 h.p. (R.A.C. rating) passenger car produced by the Standard Motor Company Ltd, of Coventry. This had an engine developing 45 h.p. with a four-speed gearbox. The Beaverette weighed about 2 tons and the maximum speed was 40 m.p.h.

A Beaverette II soon followed the Mark I and this had protection at the rear added. From the front the Mark II could be distinguished by its horizontal (instead of vertical) radiator grilles.

The armament normally consisted of a 0.303-in. Bren light machine-gun firing through a slit in the front plate. This could easily be dismounted for ground action.

Beaverettes I and II were issued during 1940 for aircraft factory defence (as originally planned), to armoured regiments waiting to be re-equipped with tanks, to the Home Guard and to the Royal Air Force for airfield protection. Then, when the Reconnaissance Corps was formed in January 1941 to carry out reconnaissance for infantry divisions, Beaverettes were issued to many battalions of this Corps for home defence and training.

The illustrations show a Beaverette I of the 53rd Battalion The Reconnaissance Corps of the 53rd (Welsh) Division as it appeared in June 1941 and a rear view of a Beaverette II of the 4th/7th Royal Dragoon Guards in July 1940. This unit had been the divisional cavalry regiment of the 2nd Infantry Division in France, where it had lost its light tanks and carriers.

Humber Ironside and Special Ironside Reconnaissance Cars

In the emergency after the Dunkirk evacuation, the Rootes Group as well as the Standard Motor Company was asked to produce a light armoured car. A prototype, known as Humberette, based on the Humber Super Snipe car chassis, was built during June 1940. This vehicle, with some slight modifications, including W.D. pattern rims for Runflat tyres, was put into production in the following month. Two hundred were built and known as Ironside I. Weighing about 2¾ tons, armoured to a maximum of 12-mm. and powered by the Humber 75/80 h.p. six-cylinder engine, these light armoured cars had a top speed of 45 m.p.h. Open-topped vehicles, they carried no fixed armament but were usually equipped with a 0.303-in. Bren light machine-gun or a 0.55-in. Boys anti-tank rifle, as available.

Ironsides were supplied to armoured regiments in lieu of tanks and subsequently to equip armoured car regiments or the Reconnaissance Corps, eventually classified as Cars, 4×2, Light Reconnaissance.

Another aspect of the defence of the United Kingdom was the need to provide safe transport for Cabinet ministers and members of the Royal Family in the event of air attack or parachute troops landing. The Ironside was selected as the most suitable type of armoured vehicle for adaptation for this purpose, after an old Lanchester armoured car had been tried out and found unsuitable. The detachment of the 12th Royal Lancers responsible for providing the escorts for the Royal Family and Cabinet Ministers received the first Humber Special Ironside armoured saloon on 13 September, 1940, followed by a second five days later, and soon afterwards both the King and Queen and the Prime Minister had travelled in these vehicles.

Although a reasonable degree of comfort was provided in the armoured saloons, they had no windows and so in the later cars built (two of which were received by the 12th Royal Lancers in December) small bullet-proof windows were provided.

Dodge Armoured Car and Bedford 30 cwt, 4 × 2, Armoured Anti-tank Lorry

The Dodge armoured vehicle was conceived by Sir Malcolm Campbell, the racing driver and in 1940 holder of the world water-speed record, and former holder of the world land-speed record. Campbell was then Officer Commanding the Provost Company of 56th (London) Division. It was arranged that Leo Villa, Campbell's Chief Racing Mechanic, should construct a prototype at his (Campbell's) private workshop in Surrey. This prototype was built on a Fordson lorry chassis, using ⅛-in. mild steel. This prototype was then handed over to Briggs Motor Bodies Ltd, of Dagenham, to produce a pilot production model in ⅞-in. or 1-in. armour plate, using the same chassis.

Within the limits of what could be done in the time and with the materials available, the Dodge Armoured Car was a well-thought-out design, with attention paid to the arrangement of the armour for the best protection and accessibility of components. The fully-enclosed hull had several ports for the operation of crew weapons such as the 0.303-in. Bren machine-gun or the 0.55-in. Boys anti-tank rifle.

The Lorry, 30 cwt, 4 × 2, Armoured Anti-tank, Bedford, was, by contrast with the Dodge Armoured

Car, a very simple improvisation on a lorry chassis. The chassis was the Bedford model OXA with a 72 h.p. six-cylinder engine, which was widely used by the British Army as a load carrier. This modification consisted of the provision of an armoured cab for the driver, behind which was mounted on the lorry platform a rectangular armoured box which constituted the fighting compartment. The only other armour was plates over the radiator and over the petrol tanks at the side. No weapons were permanently mounted but ports were provided on all sides for the operation of crew weapons and it was intended that the principal armament should be the 0.55-in. Boys anti-tank rifle, a single-shot weapon suitable for use against light armoured vehicles. A 0.303-in. Bren gun was often carried in addition to, or instead of, the anti-tank rifle.

The illustrations show a Dodge Armoured Car in the colours of one of the infantry battalions of the 47th (London) Division, one of the formations which defended southern England, and a Bedford Armoured Lorry belonging in 1941 to the 59th Battalion The Reconnaissance Corps, of the 59th Infantry Division.

T.O.G. I Heavy Tank

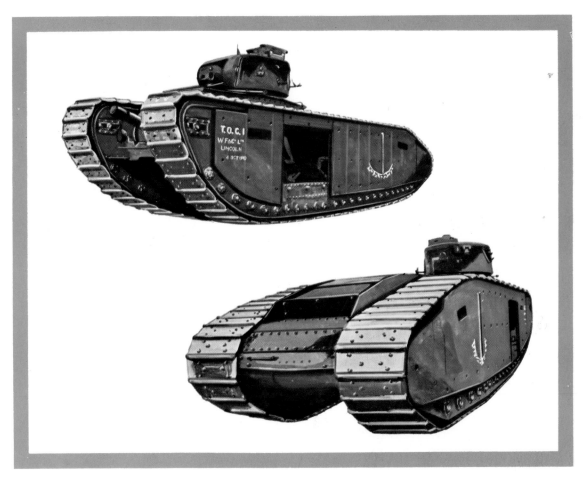

This interesting tank started life as an alternative to the A.20 (which evolved into the Churchill) as a means of breaching the German Siegfried Line defences. It was felt that the experience of the tank designers of the First World War should be drawn upon, and Sir Albert Stern, who was prominent in tank production in 1917-18, was asked to get together some of his old associates to design an assault tank. A committee was formed under Sir Albert Stern and included Sir Eustace Tennyson d'Eyncourt, Mr. H. Ricardo and General Sir Ernest Swinton and became known as 'The Old Gang', subsequently giving its initials 'TOG' to the new tank evolved in conjunction with the design staff of William Foster & Co. Ltd., who also had played a leading part in the First World War tank design and production.

The tank required was to be able to traverse shelled and waterlogged ground, to be protected against 47-mm. armour-piercing and 105-mm. high-explosive shells at 100 yards and to carry a field gun (capable of piercing 7 ft of reinforced concrete), together with armour-piercing weapons and machine-guns.

Design commenced in February 1940 and T.O.G. I was running in October, by which time its original

purpose, now that France was defeated, no longer existed. However, development was allowed to continue, if only for the sake of research into several interesting features which had been included in the design. These included a Paxman Ricardo Diesel engine of 600 h.p. (the most powerful tank engine in existence in the United Kingdom at the time) and an electric transmission and steering system. (This was later replaced by a hydraulic transmission.)

T.O.G. I as completed broadly resembled the French Char B.1 bis, which had influenced some features of its design. A 75-mm. gun was mounted in the front hull, and a Matilda turret was mounted on the hull roof. However, neither the turret armament nor the side sponsons allowed for in the design appear ever to have been fitted.

The tracks of T.O.G. I were un-sprung and with a weight of about 70 tons, not surprisingly, the maximum speed was only 8½ m.p.h., although the trench crossing ability was exceptionally good and comparable to that of the Tank Mark V** of 1918. Steering was difficult because of the exceptionally high ratio of track length to width between track centres.

A revised specification for the A.13 led, in 1939, to the London Midland and Scottish Railway being asked to abandon work on an earlier cruiser tank, which was proving unsuccessful, and take on the A.13 instead.

The A.13 Mark III, as it became known, was basically the same specification as the Cruiser Mark IVA with the 30-mm. armour basis, but it was desired to increase the effectiveness of the protection by improved ballistic shape of the armour and by lowering the height of the tank. The suspension.was to be the same as the earlier Christie Cruisers, but a new tank engine, specially designed by Meadows, was to be used.

Many difficulties developed in the design of the A.13 Mark III, which came to be known as Cruiser Mark V, to which the name Covenanter was added. These were chiefly centred on the engine, which was the only major untried feature. The cooling was the main problem and the earliest production vehicles which were running by 1940 soon had their engine air intake

louvres (sitated at the front left-hand side, next to the driver) modified in Army workshops, the resulting vehicles being known as Covenanter IIs. Two further basic Marks, Covenanter III and IV, appeared before the end of 1941 but the cooling problem was never solved really satisfactorily and the Covenanter was declared unfit for overseas service. This tank, nevertheless, played an important part in the defence of the United Kingdom, first in helping to re-equip the 1st Armoured Division, back from France, and later in contributing to the new armoured divisions being raised. The 9th Armoured Division's tanks were almost exclusively Covenanters by the end of 1941. In all, 1,771 Covenanters were built.

The illustrations both show a Covenanter of the 1st Fife and Forfar Yeomanry, one of the armoured regiments of the 28th Armoured Brigade, 9th Armoured Division, in 1941. This tank has the earlier type of axle-shaped external gun mantlet.

Cockatrice and Heavy Cockatrice Flamethrowers

The Cockatrice type of mobile flamethrower was developed during 1941 by Lagonda Ltd as a vehicle for the defence of airfields or harbours. They were based on a prototype flamethrower vehicle, using an armoured Commer lorry chassis, built by Lagonda's in the Autumn of 1940.

The Cockatrice's flame projector was mounted in a small turret on the roof of the vehicle: it used 8 gallons of fuel per second and had a range of 100 yards. Two forms of chassis were used, both lightly armoured – the 4×4 Bedford model QL and the 6×6 A.E.C. (of the type used by the R.A.F. as refuelling tenders and crane lorries). The arrangement was, however, the same for both models, the main difference being that a greater supply of fuel for the flamethrower could be carried in the heavier A.E.C. vehicle. Both types carried as supplementary armament two light machine-guns on an open anti-aircraft mounting, at the rear of the vehicle.

Sixty Bedford Cockatrices were constructed for the defence of Royal Naval airfields and six of the A.E.C. heavy Cockatrices were built for the Royal Air Force.

A General Staff specification, A.20, for a heavy infantry tank capable of breaching the defences of the German Siegfried Line, was drawn up in September 1939. This called for 60-mm. frontal protection and a speed of 10 m.p.h. Consideration was given to various forms of armament, ranging in calibre from the 2-pr (40-mm.) anti-tank gun to a low-velocity 3.7-in. (95-mm.) howitzer.

Harland & Wolff Ltd., the Belfast engineers and shipbuilders, were asked to design and supply four mild steel prototypes of A.20, or Infantry Tank Mark IV. The first of these was running by the middle of 1940 and although the armament had not been fitted its mechanical performance was disappointing, both engine and gearbox turning out to be unsatisfactory.

Vauxhall Motors Ltd., manufacturers of cars and Bedford lorries, were then asked to design a new 350 h.p. engine. This was done successfully, but it was decided to replace the A.20 specification with a revised one, A.22, in which, nevertheless, the new Bedford engine was incorporated. Vauxhall Motors,

assisted by Dr. H. E. Merritt, Director of Tank Design, undertook to design and produce the new version of Infantry Tank Mark IV.

The original armament consisted of a 2-pr gun and coaxial 7.92-mm. Besa machine-gun in the turret and a 3-in. howitzer, firing high-explosive ammunition, in the hull front, next to the driver. A second model, known at first as Tank, Infantry, Mark IVA, had a second Besa machine-gun in place of the 3-in. howitzer. When, in June 1941, names were adopted officially for British tanks, these two models became known as Churchill I and Churchill II respectively. In all, 5,640 Churchills were produced by the end of the war, of which something like 2,000 were built as Churchill I's or II's.

The illustrations show a Churchill II of the Polish Army Tank Brigade, which had begun to receive Churchill tanks in the United Kingdom by the end of 1941, and a Churchill I of the 9th Battalion Royal Tank Regiment, which formed part of one of the newly raised British Army Tank Brigades.

Crusader I and Crusader III Cruiser Tanks, Mark VI

The Crusader arose from a proposal by the Nuffield organization for a 'heavy cruiser' development of their earlier model, Cruiser Mark IV. This the War Office accepted: the pilot model was running in July 1939 and full scale production was under way in 1940.

Although the armour protection was increased to a maximum of 40-mm., an extra pair of road wheels added, the main turret redesigned and an auxiliary turret added, the Cruiser Mark VI had many features of the Cruiser Mark IV. These included the same form of Christie suspension, the 340 b.h.p. Nuffield Liberty engine and the same turret armament. Nevertheless, it proved to be far less reliable than its predecessor, particularly when subjected to desert conditions in North Africa. Mechanically, the engine fan drive and the air cleaner were particular sources of weakness, and the cramped auxiliary turret mounting a single 7.92-mm. Besa machine-gun was unsatisfactory. The Crusader's good speed of nearly 30 m.p.h. was an asset in the desert, though, and was a feature liked by its crews and admired by the Germans and Italians – the latter building an experimental tank of their own modelled on the Crusader.

The demand for heavier armour led to the introduction of the Crusader II, in which the frontal protection was increased to 49-mm. The auxiliary turret was usually omitted in this model, the aperture plated over and the space created used for extra stowage.

The 6-pr gun having by then become available, the Crusader III was designed to use it, and the first tanks of this model came off the production lines in May 1942. Basically the same turret was used, with the mantlet redesigned, but the bigger gun meant a reduction in the crew to three.

A total of 5,300 Crusaders was built by a group of firms under the parentage of Nuffield Mechanizations and Aero Limited. This total includes tanks which were later in the war converted to anti-aircraft tanks and 17-pr gun tractors and chiefly employed in action in the North West Europe campaign. The Crusader I's action was in the North African desert in 1941 and the illustration shows one in the markings used at the end of that year. Crusader III's were used by both the Eighth and First Armies in North Africa, and one belonging to a regiment of 6th Armoured Division of First Army in Tunisia in 1942 is shown.

As a successor to the Crusader, a new cruiser tank was planned in 1940 to have much heavier armour, a 6-pr gun, and to greatly improve the power/weight ratio by using a de-rated version of the Rolls-Royce Merlin aero engine. The design was completed but as the new engine could not be ready for some time, the Nuffield organization produced an interim model, known as Cruiser Mark VII (and later as Cavalier). The Cavalier was mechanically rather unreliable and only a few hundred were built. It was however, redesigned by Leyland Motors Limited, retaining the same engine modified and linked to a Merrit-Brown gearbox. The suspension was also improved, although the armour (a basic 76-mm. frontal protection) and the 6-pr gun, coaxial and hull 7.92-mm. Besa machine-gun armaments were unchanged. This tank was known as Centaur I. The British 75-mm. replaced the 6-pr gun in Centaur III, and Centaur IV was a close support version armed with the 95-mm. howitzer.

The Cromwell appeared as the natural development of the Centaur which had been designed so that the Nuffield Liberty engine could easily be replaced by the new engine, when the Meteor engine was ready for it. The first batch of Meteors (adapted from the Merlin aero engine) were built by Rolls-Royce (although other manufacturers then assumed production) and the Cromwell was produced in series from January 1943 onwards. After some changes, Leyland Motors Limited some months later became production 'parents' for the Cromwell as well as the Centaur.

Running through eight basic Marks, the Cromwells I-III had the 6-pr gun, the IV, V and VII had the 75-mm., and the VI and VIII had the 95-mm. howitzer. The early Cromwells were exceedingly fast, with a maximum speed of 40 m.p.h., but this was governed down to 32 m.p.h. on later models to lengthen the life of the Christie suspension. Welded hull construction was first used in British tanks on the Cromwell V w and VII w, and in these tanks the maximum thickness was increased from 76-mm. to 101-mm.

Challenger Cruiser Tank

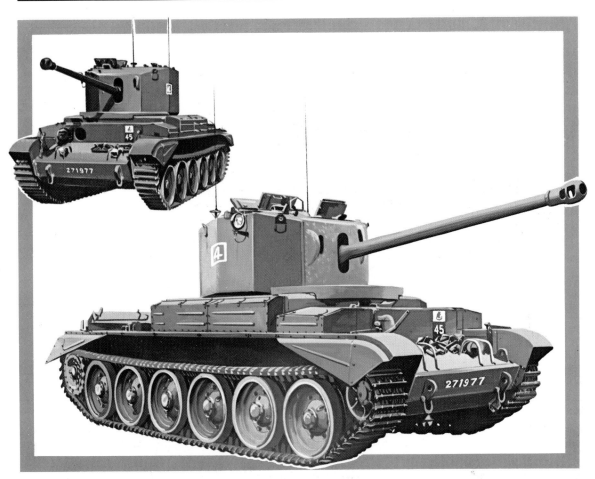

The Challenger was designed in 1942 as a cruiser tank to mount the new 17-pr gun. Prototypes were produced in the same year by the design firm, Birmingham Railway Carriage and Wagon Company, the use of many components of the Cromwell series easing many problems. Development of the turret was undertaken by Stothert and Pitt Ltd who were specialists in A.F.V. turret design. Problems were encountered during trials with the suspension and the turret and mounting, and then it was suggested that the 17-pr gun should be mounted in the Sherman, which was becoming available in increasing numbers to Britain.

The latter proved ultimately to be the best answer to the question of getting a powerful tank gun into the field where it could tackle the latest German tanks. Nevertheless, 200 Challengers were ordered and, the design snags eliminated, delivered during 1944. They were used chiefly by British regiments equipped with Cromwells in North West Europe, from Normandy onwards.

The illustrations show a tank of 8th King's Royal Irish Hussars, the armoured reconnaissance regiment of 7th Armoured Division.

The Comet was the last of the line of British cruiser tanks and by far the best. It had a good gun and was fast and reliable.

Leyland Motors Limited undertook the design of the Comet: work was commenced during 1943 and the first prototype was completed in February 1944. Designed around the new 77-mm. gun—a shorter version of the 17-pr—some of the best features of the Cromwell were used, including the same Meteor engine. All-welded construction was used for the hull and turret, a system also employed with some of the later versions of the Cromwell. The Christie suspension system was again used but in a heavier form, since the Comet's weight was about 4½-5 tons heavier than that of the Cromwell. After trials with the prototype, wider tracks were used and track return rollers (four each side) were added. A hull Besa machine-gun position like the Cromwell's was retained in the new design, and this was one point

of subsequent criticism, because of the vertical plate it needed—far more vulnerable than the sloping glacis plate of the German Panther, one of the Comet's adversaries. The hull floor protection against mines was also felt to be not fully satisfactory.

The first production Comets arrived in September 1944 and, when delivered to armoured regiments towards the end of the year, met with general approval. The 77-mm. gun did not have quite the penetrative ability of the 17-pr but was very accurate and also had good high explosive ammunition. As a result of the German offensive in the Ardennes, which interrupted training, the Comet was not used in action until after the Rhine crossing in 1945. The first formation to be re-equipped with the Comet was the 29th Armoured Brigade of 11th Armoured Division, and tanks of Regimental Headquarters, 2nd Fife and Forfar Yeomanry of this brigade are shown in the illustrations.

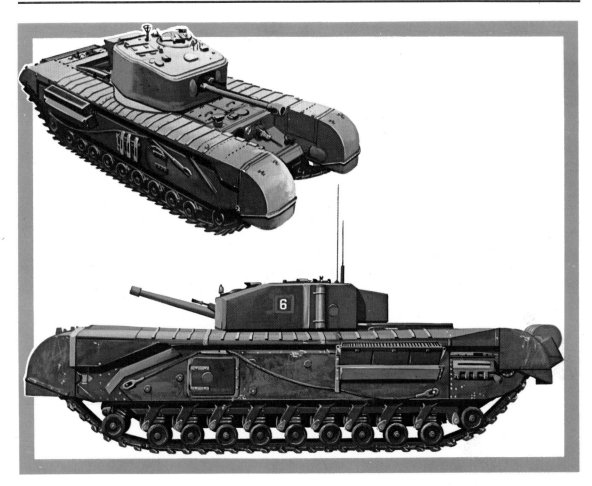

The first versions of the Infantry Tank Mark IV, to appear in 1941—the Churchills I and II—were equipped, of necessity, with 2-pr gun turrets. However, as a supply of 6-pr guns became available the Churchill III entered the production line, using a welded turret designed by Babcock and Wilcox Limited. Mechanically the same as its predecessors, having the 350 h.p. Bedford twelve-cylinder with a Merritt-Brown 4-speed gearbox, the Churchill III differed from the Churchill II mainly in the different turret and ammunition stowage. A little later, the Churchill III was joined on the production lines by a further version, Churchill IV, with the same armament but having a cast instead of a welded turret.

Some Churchill IIIs and other Marks were among the tanks supplied to the U.S.S.R. in 1942, but it was not until the Tunisian campaign of 1942-43 that the Churchill proved its worth, particularly in mountainous country.

An entirely new version of the Churchill was designed by Vauxhall Motors Limited, the original 'parent' company for the group of Churchill tank manufacturers, to meet a new War Office specification A.22F (later renumbered A.42) for an infantry tank with 6-in. frontal armour. The new model, known as Churchill VII, although superficially similar to earlier Churchills, used a completely different form of hull construction in that a hull frame was dispensed with, the armour plate itself forming the hull. Many detailed improvements were incorporated, the most obvious being circular side doors and driver's vision port instead of the rectangular variety. A commander's turret vision cupola was introduced after the first few Churchill VIIs were built. The Churchill VII had main armament of a 75-mm. gun with a coaxial 7.92-mm. Besa machine-gun and another Besa in the hull front. A close support tank, Churchill VIII, was identical except for the 95-mm. howitzer which replaced the 75-mm. gun.

Reliable, with heavy armour and a reasonably satisfactory gun, the Churchill VII (together with earlier models brought up to roughly the same standard) was one of the most important British tanks in both the Italian and North West Europe campaigns.

The illustrations show a Churchill III of 142nd (Suffolk) Regiment, Royal Armoured Corps, at the time of the Tunisian campaign, and a Churchill VII in the colours of 6th (Guards) Tank Brigade.

The war in the North African desert emphasized the need for both increased mobility and protection for field and anti-tank artillery. The Bishop was designed hurriedly in 1941 in response to an urgent request from the Middle East for a self-propelled mounting for the 25-pr field gun—a weapon that had often been found to be the only effective answer to the German medium tanks. Designed by the Birmingham Railway Carriage and Wagon Company Limited, the sturdy and reliable Valentine tank chassis was used as the carrier for the 25-pr gun, which was mounted in a fixed shield with a total traverse of 8 degrees, elevation of 15 degrees and depression of 5 degrees.

One hundred Bishops were built by July 1942, and nearly all of them were used in North Africa.

The Bishop design was proposed as the basis of a self-propelled mounting for the new 17-pr anti-tank gun in 1942, but this was found to be impracticable. Nevertheless, the Valentine chassis was again used but this time with a rearward-facing layout for the gun. The rear-facing arrangement of the 17-pr gun in the Archer permitted a compact design—particularly useful in an anti-tank gun—and a total traverse of

45 degrees allowed reasonable flexibility in use. The welded upper hull had armour protection up to 20 mm.—effective against small arms. A 0.30-in. Browning machine-gun was carried for protection against local ground attack and aircraft.

The Bishop used the Valentine II chassis with an A.E.C. 131 b.h.p. diesel engine, but the Archer chassis was equivalent to that of the later models of Valentine tank with the General Motors diesel of 192 b.h.p., giving a top speed of 20 m.p.h. – compared with the slightly heavier Bishop's 15 m.p.h.

Although the merits (rapid withdrawal in emergency, for one) and demerits of the rearward-facing gun were often debated, the Archer was generally acknowledged as reliable and the effectiveness of the 17-pr gun was never in doubt. The Archer was used by anti-tank regiments in North West Europe and Italy from 1944 onwards, and continued to be employed by the British Army for several years after the war. An Archer of the anti-tank regiment of 15th (Scottish) Division in Germany in 1945 is shown in the illustration. The Bishop shown is as it appeared in the Sicily campaign in 1943.

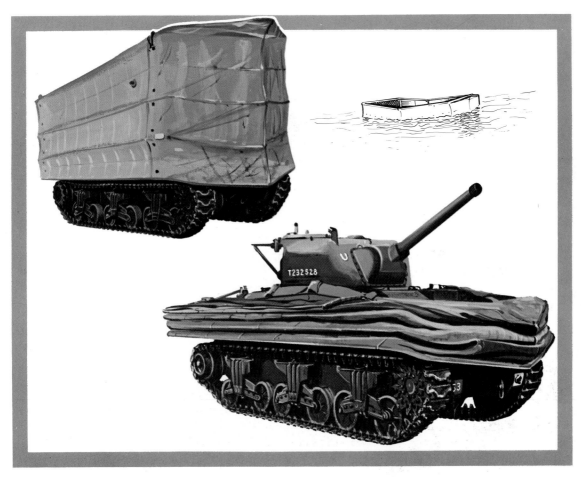

One of the most ingenious, yet basically simple, devices of World War II was Nicholas Straussler's D.D. amphibious tank. By water-proofing the hull and raising the freeboard, it was found that an ordinary tank could be made to float without the necessity for the clumsy buoyancy chambers or pontoons, or a boat type of hull as used in earlier amphibious tanks. The means used by Straussler to increase the freeboard was to add a canvas screen around the edge of the hull. Tried out first on a 7½-ton Light Tank Mark VII in 1941, the screen was raised by means of inflatable rubber tubes and held erect by metal struts. Production of 625 D.D. tanks based on the 17-ton Valentine tank then took place and deliveries were made in 1943-44. It was, however, desired to extend the use of the D.D. device to the Sherman, virtually the standard medium tank used by the British Army, and Sherman D.D. prototypes were built and proved as successful as the earlier model.

As in earlier D.D. tanks, the Sherman had Duplex Drive (hence the initials)—normal propulsion on tracks on land and propellers for movement on water. The tracks of the Sherman were also run in water because

the power take off to drive the twin 3-bladed propellers was implemented through stub axles on the rear idler wheels. The propellers were movable for steering, which was operated by the tank commander through either mechanical linkage to the propellers or a hydraulic system.

The water speed of the Sherman D.D. was up to 6 m.p.h. and, as the tracks were running all the time the tank was afloat, it could climb ashore the moment it touched ground. The screens could be lowered quickly, and the Sherman's armament, a 75-mm. gun and a 0.30-in. Browning in the turret (the hull machine-gun had had to be eliminated in the D.D.) used.

A tactical surprise was achieved with the first use of Sherman D.D. tanks in action on some Normandy beaches in 1944, because in the water they were not immediately recognized as tanks. They were also used later on in the Italian campaign (together with a small number of Valentine D.D.s) and at the Rhine crossing in March 1945.

The illustrations show a Sherman D.D. (with screens folded) of 4th Armoured Brigade in Germany in 1945, a Sherman D.D. afloat, on land with the screens raised.

The anti-mine flail was a power-driven revolving drum to which rows of heavy chains were attached which, beating the ground in front of the vehicle to which the device was fitted, exploded mines on contact.

The Mechanical Experimental Establishment in the Middle East first fitted the device to a lorry and then, after trials, to a Matilda tank. This equipment was then called Matilda Scorpion Mark I.

The flails of the Matilda Scorpion I were made up of wire cable to the ends of which short lengths of chain were attached. The rotating drum was driven by a Ford V-8 engine, mounted in an armoured box on the right-hand side of the tank's hull. A cardan shaft took the transmission along the supporting girder to a bevel box and from it to the rotor. The flail engine was operated by an extra crew member who had the unenviable job of sitting at the rear of the armoured box behind the engine. In this position he was nearly choked by dust and fumes from the flail engine.

An order for twenty-four Matilda Scorpion Mark Is was completed in time for them to be used to help clear minefields for the Battle of Alamein in October 1942.

Still beset by mechanical difficulties and with a flailing speed of only ½ m.p.h., nevertheless the Scorpions were considered reasonably satisfactory. A better version in which the flail operator was carried in the tank itself, and the design of the side girder was changed and other improvements effected, was known as the Matilda Scorpion Mark II and was ready by early 1943.

In order to take advantage of the greater mobility of the American Grant, the Scorpion Mark II flail equipment was adapted to this tank, the combination being known as Grant Scorpion Mark III. The hull-mounted 75-mm. gun had to be removed, but the 37-mm. gun turret could be retained although this was also, in fact, removed when it was necessary to reduce the overall dimensions to be carried in landing craft. Grant Scorpions were used in the Sicily campaign in the Summer of 1943.

The final developments of the flail tank were the Grant Scorpion IV and the Sherman Scorpion. The former used two Dodge engines, mounted at the rear of the hull, driving the rotating drum by means of cardan shafts each side.

Sherman Crab I and Crab II

The first U.K. flail tank, known as Baron, used the Matilda chassis. Early models had one engine to drive the flail but the final model had two flail engines. Sixty were built in 1943 for training purposes. The next type, the Valentine Scorpion, was based on designs received from the Middle East, although the rotor was like that of the Baron. Again, only a small order (150 vehicles) for training only was given.

Next, flail development was transferred to the Sherman tank—this had the advantage of using the same basic vehicle that was to equip many British armoured regiments.

Prototypes of three models were built in 1943, the Sherman Marquis, turretless and based on the Baron and Scorpion; the Sherman Pram Scorpion, retaining its turret and taking its flail drive from the tank's main engines; and the Sherman Crab. The latter was considered to be the best design and was the one adopted for production in quantity for employment in the forthcoming campaign in North West Europe.

Fitted to the Sherman V, powered by a Chrysler thirty-cylinder 350 b.h.p. engine, the flail was operated through a power take off on the right-hand side of the hull, leading through a universal-jointed cardan shaft to a bevel gear at the rotor. The rotor arms could be lifted by hydraulic rams to make transport in landing craft etc. easier. A lane 9 ft 9 in. wide could be cleared of mines at a maximum speed of 1¼ m.p.h.

A later model, Sherman Crab II (which did not become available until nearly the end of the war) was developed to overcome the fault of Crab I and all other earlier flail tanks, in that mines buried in hollows in the ground could be passed over without being detonated because the flails operated at a constant height above a level surface. The left-hand hydraulic lifting ram was replaced by a counter weight attached to the rear end of the rotor arm. This enabled the rotor arm and bearing chains to maintain a constant height over the contours of the ground.

The illustrations show a Sherman Crab I with the rotor arm at beating height (attachments on the rear of the hull are station-keeping-lights—for the benefit of following vehicles—mounted above the box containing markers to indicate the swept lane) and a Sherman Crab II flailing in a depression in the ground.

Churchill A.V.R.E. Carpet-layer and S.B.G. Bridge Carrier

The Dieppe Raid of 1942, in which heavy losses were sustained by both armour and infantry, chiefly because the tanks were unable to penetrate inland, indicated the need for protection for engineers working to surmount or destroy obstacles. A suggestion by Lieutenant J. J. Denovan, of the Royal Canadian Engineers, that a tank should be adapted for this purpose was followed up by the R.C.E. using a Churchill tank. The prototype with rearranged stowage was ready by December 1942 and a spigot motor, developed separately, was ready by February 1943 and mounted in the modified turret. The spigot motor, known as Petard, could throw a 40-lb projectile (containing a 26-lb charge) up to an extreme range of 230 yards, and was capable of destroying concrete obstacles.

The Assault Vehicle, Royal Engineers, or A.V.R.E. as it was usually called, was adjudged successful after trials and modifications to the original design which took place in 1943, and production was ordered. The Churchill III or IV was used as the basis, and a total of about 700 A.V.R.E.s was built by 1945.

Most production A.V.R.E.s were fitted with brackets on the hull for the attachment of fittings for special tasks. One of these fitments was the carpet-layer device for crossing soft patches on beaches, for example. The carpet—the most common form was hessian matting reinforced by steel tubes—was carried on a large bobbin at the front of the A.V.R.E. and was unwound by the vehicle itself running over it. A number of these were employed on the D-Day landing beaches. There were several versions, and the Carpetlayer Type D (waterproofed for landing from a landing craft) is shown in the illustration.

Another important use of the A.V.R.E. was as a carrier for the Small Box Girder (S.B.G.) bridge, which could carry a 40-ton load (the weight of a Churchill tank) over a 30-ft span. This could be laid mechanically under fire.

The A.V.R.E. was used in action in Italy and in North West Europe. Three Assault Regiments, Royal Engineers, under the command of 79th Armoured Division, with A.V.R.E.s and a variety of fitments, took part in many actions from D-Day onwards. An A.V.R.E. with S.B.G. bridge as it appeared in the attack on the Le Havre fortifications is illustrated.

Churchill A.R.V. Mark I and Sherman B.A.R.V.

Early in 1942, a Royal Electrical and Mechanical Engineers experimental section undertook the design of armoured recovery vehicles on tank chassis. The idea was to use adaptations as A.R.V.s of the same kinds of tanks used by the armoured regiments, in so far as the basic chassis was suitable for use also as a recovery vehicle. The three most important A.R.V. types which emerged were based on the Cromwell, Sherman and Churchill, corresponding with the principal tanks in use from 1943 onwards.

The Churchill A.R.V., Mark I, was a turretless vehicle carrying a 3-ton jib. This was stowed on the hull for travelling but was mounted between the front 'horns' when in use and was capable of lifting out tank engines or other major assemblies for maintenance and repair. A 100-ft length of heavy steel cable was carried for hauling out bogged-down A.F.V.s and a pulley block and ground anchors were available for indirect or difficult recovery jobs. The A.R.V. also carried a 4½-in. vice and oxy-acetylene and welding

plant among its equipment.

Development of an A.R.V. to recover disabled tanks or vehicles, both in the water and on the beaches, was commenced in 1943 specially for the forthcoming invasion of Europe. The diesel-engined Sherman III was finally selected as the standard chassis for the Beach Armoured Recovery Vehicle (B.A.R.V.). Fully waterproofed and able to operate in up to 10 feet of water, the Sherman B.A.R.V. was intended only for simple recovery operations, such as towing vehicles 'drowned' in landing from landing craft or pushing off stranded landing craft, for which wooden railway sleepers mounted on the front were provided.

The Sherman B.A.R.V.s well served their purpose in 1944 by helping to keep the D-Day beaches clear. One landed in error at a very early stage of the invasion and was taken to be a new 'secret weapon'.

The illustrations show a Churchill A.R.V., Mark I, belonging to the 3rd (Tank) Battalion Scots Guards, and a standard Sherman B.A.R.V.

UNITED KINGDOM and AUSTRALIA

Universal Carrier Mark II and Carrier 2-pr, Tank Attack (Aust.)

The British Army's demand for tracked carriers of the Bren and Scout types, and for a variety of functions, remained high throughout World War II, but even by 1940 the need was felt to standardize the design as far as possible. This resulted in the introduction of the Carrier, Universal. Mechanically the same as the earlier carriers, the Universal was powered by a Ford V-8 engine which drove the tracks via rear sprockets. Steering was by lateral displacement of the front bogie unit for gentle turns, with track braking for more abrupt turns. Although the driver's and gunner's compartments were very much the same in all carriers, the position of the armoured rear compartment varied. In the Universal Carrier, the whole of the rear was armoured, providing an open-top compartment on either side of the engine.

The Mark II version of the Universal Carrier included some improvements, such as a spare road wheel as a standard fitting, a large kit box on the rear of the hull, and either one or two footstep brackets each side of the hull. Some further improvements were incorporated in the Mark III Carrier.

Some 40,000 or more Carriers of the Universal and later associated types were built in the United Kingdom alone during World War II but, even so, it was felt necessary that Commonwealth countries should also undertake the production of tracked carriers. In Canada 29,000 of the Universal-type were built to a similar specification to the U.K. version (about 5,000 of the larger Windsor carriers were also built in Canada and the U.S.A. produced 14,000 T.16 series Carriers). A Carrier, Universal, Mark II, belonging to an infantry battalion of 43rd (Wessex) Division is illustrated.

In Australia and New Zealand carriers were also built. The earliest N.Z. carriers were built from plans sent from the United Kingdom, although later models were more like the Australian ones. Australian production was much greater, to meet the heavier demand in that country, and the basic U.K. carrier design was simplified mechanically in that the track displacement device for steering was omitted. Although in other respects broadly the same as the U.K. carriers, the later Australian carriers had a modified hull with a sloping glacis plate.

Humber Armoured Cars Mark III and Mark IV

Humber Armoured Cars were numerically the most important British-built armoured cars of World War II, well over 5,000 being produced by the Rootes Group between 1940 and 1945.

The earliest Humber Armoured Car, the Mark I, was almost identical externally to the Guy Mark IA Armoured Car, and its mechanical layout although based, of course, on Rootes components was on similar lines to that of the Guy. Service experience suggested improvements and a cleaned-up front end, incorporating the driver's visor in the glacis plate, and radiator intake improvements were introduced in the Mark II.

The Armoured Car, Humber Mark III, which entered production in 1942 had a more roomy turret than the Marks I-II, which allowed the crew to be increased to four. The first three Marks of Humber Armoured Car all had an armament of two Besa machine-guns, one of

7.92-mm. calibre and the other 15-mm. The latter was never an entirely satisfactory weapon, being prone to stoppages, and in the Humber Mark IV Armoured Car the American 37-mm. gun was introduced in its place. Because this reduced the turret space available, the crew was reduced to three men.

All the Humber Armoured Cars weighed about 7 tons and their 90 b.h.p. six-cylinder engines gave them a top speed of 45 m.p.h. They were used by both armoured car regiments (where they tended to be used at regimental and squadron headquarters if Daimlers were also available) and Reconnaissance Regiments (of infantry divisions) in most theatres of war in which British and Commonwealth troops were engaged up to the end of the war. The illustrations show a Mark III as it appeared in the North African desert about 1942, and a Mark IV of 1st Reconnaissance Regiment in Italy in 1944.

Daimler Armoured Cars Mark I and Mark II

Inspired to a large extent by the design of the Car, Scout Mark I, the Daimler Armoured Car was built to the 'Tank, Light, Wheeled' formula of a wheeled vehicle having performance, armour and armament comparable to that of contemporary light tanks. After some initial difficulties it turned out to be one of the best armoured cars of World War II.

The mechanical layout of the Daimler Armoured Car consisted of a rear-mounted, 95 b.h.p. six-cylinder engine from which the transmission was taken via a 'Fluid Flywheel' and pre-selector gearbox to a centrally mounted transfer box with a single differential. From this the power was transmitted via four parallel driving shafts and Tracta universal joints to each wheel, with final reduction gears in each hub. This arrangement helped to keep the height down, as there were no central transmission shafts, and a further point making for compact design was that all the automotive components were attached direct to the hull, there being no chassis as such. Two other interesting features were the early use of disc brakes, and the inclusion of a second steering wheel facing the rear, together with basic driving controls, to enable the

car to be driven rapidly in reverse in emergency.

The armament of the Daimler Armoured Car was identical to that of the Tetrarch Light Tank (with which it shared the turret design), a 2-pr gun and coaxially mounted 7.92-mm. Besa machine-gun.

Some improvements suggested by experience in service of the Daimler Mark I were incorporated in the Mark II, which followed the Mark I into production towards the latter end of the war. The most important changes were a 2-speed dynamo, a driver's escape hatch in the hull roof, an improved gun mantlet, and a different radiator and grill. Both Marks of Daimler (a total of 2,694 of which was built) sometimes had Littlejohn Adaptors added to the 2-pr guns, which greatly increased their penetrative ability.

The Daimler Mark I Armoured Car was first used in action in North Africa in 1942, and subsequently with the Mark II in Europe and the Far East. Many British and Commonwealth armoured car regiments used these cars and the illustrations show a Mark I of the 1st Derbyshire Yeomanry (6th Armoured Division) in Tunisia, and a Mark II of 11th Hussars (7th Armoured Division) in Germany in 1945.

A.E.C. Armoured Cars Mark II and Mark III

The original A.E.C. Armoured Car (Mark I) was conceived by the Associated Equipment Company Limited in 1941 as a heavy armoured car with both armour and armament equivalent to that of a cruiser tank and, in fact, used the 2-pr turret of a Valentine tank. This private venture was successful and 122 of them were built, many being sent to North Africa in 1942. When British tank armament increased, the A.E.C. Mark II Armoured Car was designed to use the 6-pr gun (with a coaxial 7.92-mm. Besa machine-gun) and, at the same time, the opportunity was taken to redesign the shape of the front hull and introduce other improvements. The Mark II had a more powerful A.E.C. diesel engine of 158 b.h.p. (which gave a top speed of 41 m.p.h.) and a crew of four. It weighed 12.7 tons and the armour protection was at a maximum of 30-mm.

The next step, in the Mark III, was to substitute the British 75-mm. gun for the 6-pr. The Mark III was very similar to its predecessor in most other respects, except that it had two (rather than one) electric fans installed in the turret roof. A total of 507 Armoured Cars, A.E.C. Marks II and III was built.

Some A.E.C. Mark IIs were supplied to the Yugoslav partisans in 1944 and one of these is shown in the smaller illustration. A.E.C. Mark IIIs were used principally in the Heavy Troops of British Armoured Car Regiments in the North West Europe campaign, and a car of 2nd Household Cavalry Regiment (then in VIII Corps) is illustrated.

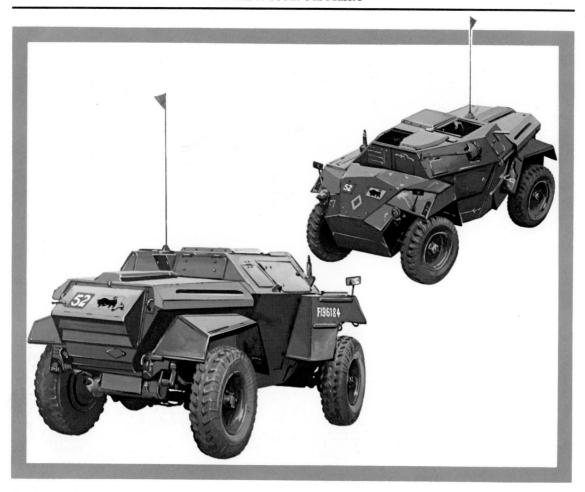

Production of the Daimler Scout Car (introduced into service at the beginning of World War II) was continued throughout the war. Only relatively minor changes were made in the design because it was a highly successful vehicle. However, as the number built could not meet the demand, the Rootes Group was asked to design and manufacture a scout car to supplement the Daimler Scout Cars.

To avoid unnecessary production complications the Rootes Group design which became known as Car, Scout, Humber, Mark I, employed a high proportion of components used in existing Humber 4-wheel drive military vehicles, such as the Light Reconnaissance Car, but adapted for a rear engine layout. The ubiquitous Rootes 87 b.h.p. six-cylinder engine was linked to a 4-speed gearbox and gave a top speed of

60 m.p.h. Rather larger than the Daimler Scout Car and with room for three men, the Humber Scout Car was of a mechanically less sophisticated design, and the maximum frontal protection was only 14-mm. compared with the Daimler's 30-mm. For some or all of these reasons, given a choice, armoured regiments tended to use Humbers for liaison purposes rather than scouting.

The Mark II version of the Humber Scout Car was externally similar to the Mark I but had synchromesh added to 2nd gear as well as in 3rd and 4th. A total of 4,300 Humber Scout Cars were built between about late 1942 and the end of the war.

The illustrations show vehicles belonging to 11th Armoured Division.

Humber 4 × 4 Light Reconnaissance Car Mark IIIA and Morris 4 × 4 Light Reconnaissance Car Mark II

The Rootes Group were responsible for the major part of the production of Light Reconnaissance cars in the United Kingdom in World War II (3,600 in total), commencing with the Mark I (known as Ironside I) of 1940. This was followed by the Mark II which had an enclosed roof mounting a small turret, and in turn by the externally similar Mark III. This model, however, introduced 4-wheel drive. It was succeeded in 1942 by the Mark IIIA, shown here, which had various minor improvements, the most noticeable of which were extra observation ports at the front corner angles of the hull. A 3½-ton vehicle powered by an 87 b.h.p. Humber six-cylinder engine, which gave it a top speed of 50 m.p.h., the armament of the Humber Mark IIIA Light Reconnaissance Car consisted normally of a 0.303-in. Bren light machine-gun mounted in the turret, to which was sometimes added a 0.55-in. Boys anti-tank rifle usually mounted in the hull front. Often a smoke discharger was also carried. The car had a crew of three, and light armour of up to 10-mm.

The Car, 4 × 2, Light Reconnaissance, Morris, Mark I was put into production by the Nuffield Group to supplement the Humbers and the later versions of the Beaverette being built by the Standard Motor Company. A rear-engined vehicle, the Morris Mark I's cross-country performance was enhanced by the smooth enclosed design of its underbelly. Nevertheless, a 4-wheel drive version, the Mark II, was introduced to take the place of the Mark I. With a 71.8 b.h.p. Morris engine and weighing slightly more at 3.7 tons and with 14-mm. armour, the specification and performance of the Morris Mark II was similar to that of the Humber Mark IIIA.

Intended originally as equipment for the Reconnaissance Corps, both the Morris and Humber Light Reconnaissance Cars were also used extensively by armoured car units of the Royal Air Force Regiment, and the Humber Mark IIIA in the illustration is one belonging to the R.A.F. Regiment in the North West Europe campaign. Both makes of car were used also for reconnoitring and liaison purposes by Royal Engineers field companies and the Morris Mark II shown is in the markings of a field company, R.E., of the 43rd (Wessex) Infantry Division.

A.E.C. Armoured Command Vehicle 4 × 4 Mark I and A.E.C. Armoured Command Vehicle 6 × 6 Mark I

The A.E.C. Matador chassis was used as the basis of the 4-wheeled A.C.V. – known at first officially as 'Lorry, 3 ton, 4 × 4, Armoured Command, A.E.C.' This consisted basically of an armoured body (12-mm. armour) fitted out internally for command purposes and carrying two wireless sets. These were a No. 19 H.P. and a No. 19 in the Low Power version, and an R.C.A. receiver and a No. 19 set in the High Power version.

Weighing nearly 12 tons, the A.E.C. 4 × 4 Armoured Command Vehicle was powered by an A.E.C. diesel engine of 95 b.h.p. which gave it a top speed of 35 m.p.h. No armament was fitted but a Bren light machine-gun was carried for defence.

A total of 416 4 × 4 A.C.V.s was built, and these were supplemented in 1944-45 by 151 vehicles of a new model – on an A.E.C. 6-wheel-drive chassis. This was very much more roomy than its predecessor, being 6 feet longer, but slightly lower. It was also very much heavier at 19 tons loaded, and was powered by a more powerful A.E.C. diesel engine of 135 b.h.p. The vehicle was divided internally, the front compartment being for staff and the rear for the wireless equipment. As in

all the earlier vehicles, eight men were carried.

The A.E.C. 4 × 4 armoured command vehicles were first used in action in the North African campaign, where, incidentally, three were captured and used by German generals, two of them by Rommel himself and his staff. These two vehicles were nicknamed 'Max' and 'Moritz', although the type was given the generic name of Mammut (Mammoth) by the Germans.

The armoured command vehicles were large and conspicuous and, of course, as they carried senior officers, valuable targets, so Major Jasper Maskelyne (a well-known stage magician in civilian life) commanding a camouflage unit of the Royal Engineers, was asked to design special camouflage for them. What he did was to disguise them as ordinary lorries, similar to the standard A.E.C. Matador gun tractors which were widely used by the British Army. This involved black shadow painting on various parts of the hull, the addition of a canvas cover to the top surfaces and an extension to the armoured noseplate. This disguise is shown in the illustration of an A.E.C. 4 × 4 A.C.V. in North Africa.

A.E.C. 6-pr Deacon Gun Carrier Mark I and Straussler S.P. 17-pr Gun

The 6-pr gun was the best British weapon available for tackling German tanks in early 1942, and the Deacon was designed as a means of increasing its mobility, chiefly for use in the North African theatre of war. The 6-pr (on a field-type, not a tank mounting) was mounted on a turntable, with a light shield open only at the rear, and carried on an armoured A.E.C. Matador chassis. The Deacon weighed 12 tons and powered by an A.E.C. six-cylinder 95 b.h.p. diesel engine had a top speed of only 19 m.p.h. Despite their bulk and slowness, the Deacons did good work in the North African campaign, after which they were handed over to the Turkish Government. A total of 150 was built in 1942 and they were supplied ex-works already painted in a bright sand yellow. A further twenty-five vehicles without the gun and a platform body were built as armoured ammunition carriers.

In 1943, an experimental wheeled self-propelled mounting for the new and very much more powerful 17-pr anti-tank gun was designed by Nicholas Straussler. Entirely original in concept, the 17-pr gun with split trail was, in effect, added to a rectangular skeleton chassis. A motive unit, consisting of Bedford type QL lorry components, was added, the engine (at the right-hand side of the chassis) driving the two front wheels for transport. When the gun was in position, the two rear wheels could be swivelled until they were at right angles to the front wheels. The right-hand rear wheel could then be driven through a power take-off from the engine, so enabling the whole carriage to be rotated through 360 degrees. Sometimes known as Monitor, the Straussler S.P. 17-pr was not adopted for service because it was felt that the mounting offered insufficient protection for the gun and its crew. The illustration shows the vehicle in its travelling position.

Ejection Charge   Smoke Canisters

The British 25 pounder field gun, one of the most versatile weapons of its class. On the left, a cut-away view of a smoke shell; below, the gun hooked up to its ammunition trailer.

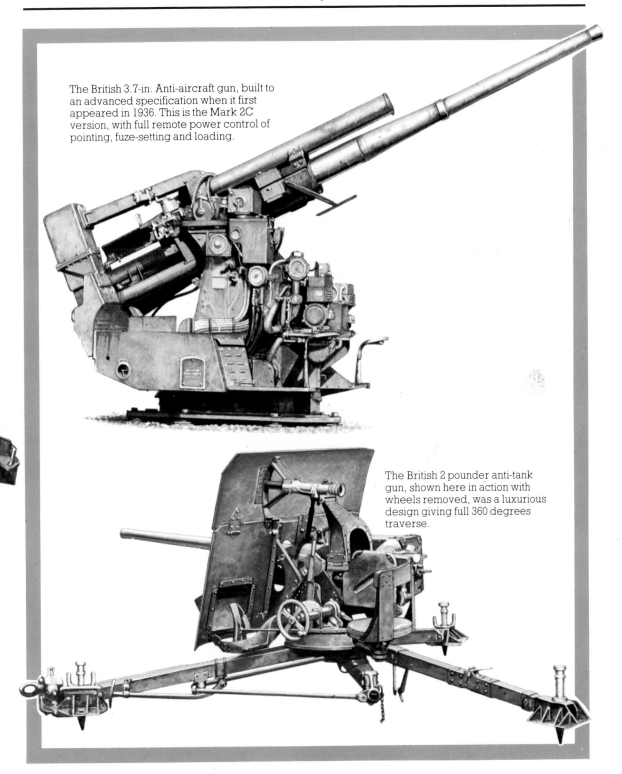

The British 3.7-in. Anti-aircraft gun, built to an advanced specification when it first appeared in 1936. This is the Mark 2C version, with full remote power control of pointing, fuze-setting and loading.

The British 2 pounder anti-tank gun, shown here in action with wheels removed, was a luxurious design giving full 360 degrees traverse.

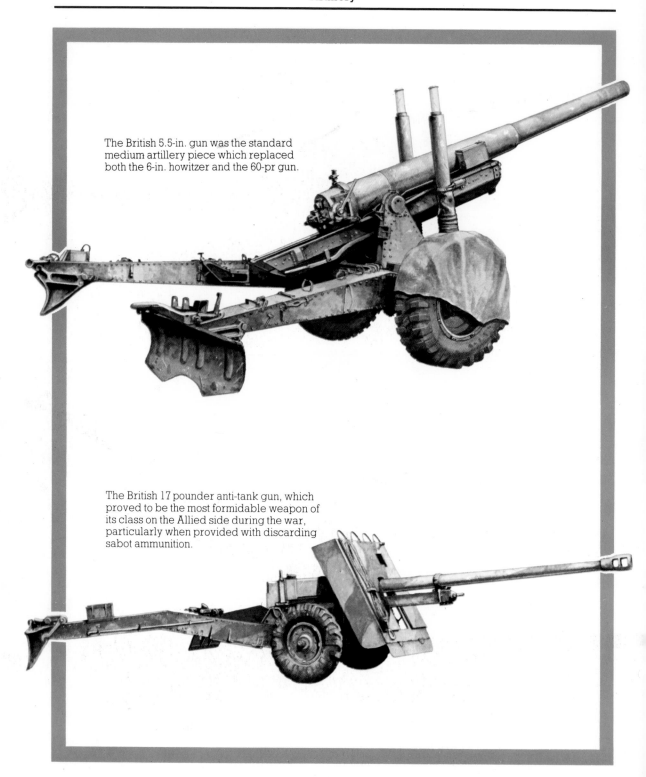

The British 5.5-in. gun was the standard medium artillery piece which replaced both the 6-in. howitzer and the 60-pr gun.

The British 17 pounder anti-tank gun, which proved to be the most formidable weapon of its class on the Allied side during the war, particularly when provided with discarding sabot ammunition.

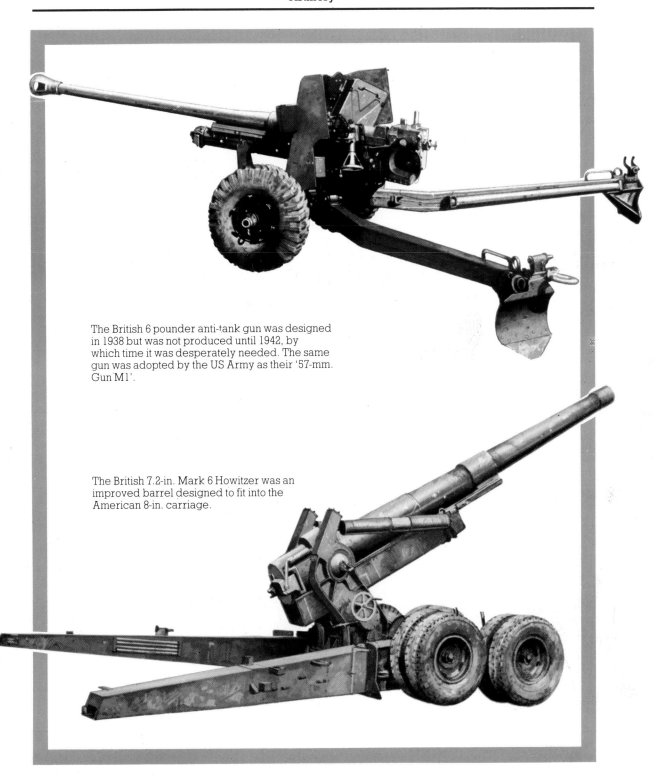

The British 6 pounder anti-tank gun was designed in 1938 but was not produced until 1942, by which time it was desperately needed. The same gun was adopted by the US Army as their '57-mm. Gun M1'.

The British 7.2-in. Mark 6 Howitzer was an improved barrel designed to fit into the American 8-in. carriage.

In 1939 the latest of a line of light tanks developed from 1933 onwards, the M2A4 was the first to carry a 37-mm. gun. This light tank also had the distinction of being one of the very earliest types of fighting vehicle to be supplied to Britain by the U.S.A., a small batch being shipped in 1941.

Powered by a 250 h.p. seven-cylinder Continental radial engine (a modified aero engine), giving a top speed of 37 m.p.h., armoured to a 25.4-mm. maximum and equipped with the 37-mm. gun, which was not greatly inferior to the British 2-pr as an armour-piercing weapon, the M2A4 was much better than contemporary British light tanks and comparable with some cruiser tanks. The secondary armament, in addition to the turret coaxial 0.30-in. Browning machine-gun, included two further Brownings in sponsons at either side of the driver's and co-driver's

positions and another in the glacis plate. Some or all of these hull-mounted machine-guns were often removed in the tanks in British service.

The suspension consisted of two two-wheeled bogie units each side, each unit sprung on vertical volute springs. The idler wheel was at the rear, off the ground, and the drive sprocket at the front.

A total of 365 M2A4s was built. A few were used in action with U.S. forces in the Pacific theatre in 1942. Those delivered to Britain in 1941 (only about forty or so) were used for Home Defence and training, in which role they were useful for familiarising the troops with the similar but improved M3 Light Tank.

The illustrations show an M2A4 supplied to Britain that was subscribed for by the Canadian town of Saskatoon, and an M2A4 of the U.S. 70th Armoured Regiment.

M3A1 Scout Car

Designed as a reconnaissance vehicle for the U.S. mechanised cavalry, the M3A1 Scout Car, built by the White Motor Company, was the last in line of a series of vehicles developed from 1929 onwards. A large, open-topped armoured vehicle, with protection ranging from 6-mm. to 12-mm., the M3A1 was powered by a 110 h.p. Hercules six-cylinder engine which gave it a maximum speed of 55-60 m.p.h. Sufficient petrol was carried for a range of 250 miles and cross-country performance with four-wheel drive was fairly good: a roller mounted at the front assisted in surmounting obstacles.

Introduced into service with the U.S. Army in mid-1939, the M3A1 Scout Car was one of the first types of armoured vehicle to be supplied in 1941 by the United States to the United Kingdom. The American vehicles, although designated Scout Cars, did not correspond in size, manoeuvrability or performance to the British requirement for a scout car, although some appear temporarily to have been used as such by

some units in the United Kingdom awaiting supplies of Daimler Scout Cars. However, good use was made by the British Army of White Scout Cars, as they were usually called, as armoured personnel carriers (they carried eight men and were were used chiefly in motor battalions of armoured divisions), as command vehicles and as armoured ambulances. Later the designation of Truck, 15 cwt., Personnel (White M3A1) was adopted by the War Office.

In American use, the armament usually consisted of a 0.5-in. M2 machine-gun (Browning) on a skate mounting travelling on a rail round the inside of the hull, and one or two 0.3-in. Browning machine-guns. These guns rarely seem to have been fitted in British-used vehicles in which, also, the front roller was often removed.

One illustration shows a Scout Car M3A1 of the U.S. Army; this has the canvas hood up. The other view is of a White Scout Car as used by the motor battalion (infantry) of a British armoured brigade in 1941.

Howitzer Motor Carriage Light Tank M.5A1 and 75-mm. M.8.

The Cadillac Division of the General Motors Corporation entered into tank production early in 1942 with a new version of the M.3 Light Tank, known as the M.5. This tank, at the suggestion of Cadillac's, was powered by two eight-cylinder V-form Cadillac automobile engines, with Cadillac Hydramatic automatic transmission. A prototype was constructed in October 1941 by conversion of a standard M.3 and after a highly successful five-hundred mile demonstration drive, the design, subject to modifications in detail, was accepted. A total of 2,074 was built by the end of 1942, when the M.5 was succeeded by an improved model M.5A1. This tank was distinguished from the M.5 chiefly by a turret with an extension at the rear for radio. Other improvements included an escape hatch in the floor of the hull, a gun mount including a direct sight telescope, extra turret periscopes and an anti-aircraft machine-gun mount on the right-hand side of the turret protected by a curved armoured shield. The latter, however, was invariably

removed on M.5A1s supplied to the British Army (by whom they were known as Stuart VIs) and sometimes, also, on U.S. Army vehicles. Production of the M.5A1 was ended in mid-1944 when 6,810 had been built.

The M.5A1 (and the M.5) was similar in most respects to the earlier M.3. It had a similar overall performance, in spite of being some 2 tons heavier, with thicker armour, but was much easier to drive than the M.3. The armament consisted of a 37-mm. gun with a coaxial 0.30-in. Browning machine-gun and another in the hull front, together with the anti-aircraft machine-gun already mentioned. An M.5A1 of the U.S. Marine Corps in the Pacific theatre of war is shown.

A variant of the M.5 light tank was the Howitzer Motor Carriage M.8. This used the same chassis with the upper hull modified to take an open-topped turret with full traverse, mounting a 75-mm. howitzer.

Known as General Scott, 1,778 M.8s were built between 1942 and 1944 and issued as close support vehicles in U.S. Headquarters companies.

Lee and Grant Medium Tank M.3

The M.3 in its original (and, numerically, by far the most important) version was powered by a Continental nine-cylinder radial air-cooled engine of 340 b.h.p. and the hull was of all-riveted construction to a maximum armour thickness of 50-mm. The engine was at the rear, the transmission being led forward to a gear-box alongside the driver and the track drive was via front sprockets. The hull-mounted 75-mm. gun at the right had a total traverse of 30 degrees and 46 rounds were carried. The turret had a full 360 degree traverse and besides the 37-mm. gun (for which 178 rounds were carried) it had a 0.30-in. Browning machine-gun, coaxially mounted. Standard M.3s also had a further Browning in the cupola on the main turret and two more in the glacis plate at the left, operated by the driver. These hull machine-guns were normally removed in all British-used vehicles and, of course, the Grant did not have the machine-gun cupola, although an anti-aircraft machine-gun was sometimes mounted on the turret.

The M.3s suspension used the horizontal volute system, already well tried in earlier medium and light tanks. It consisted of three twin-wheel bogie units each side.

The Medium M.3 first saw action (as the Grant) with the British forces in the Western Desert in the spring of 1942. In spite of its design shortcomings, its effective 75-mm. gun mounted in a reliable vehicle with a good degree of mobility (maximum speed 26 m.p.h.) helped considerably to redress the balance against the German armour. A Grant of the 3rd Royal Tank Regiment, one of the first units to receive them, is shown in one of the illustrations.

The U.S. Army also used the M.3 in action in North Africa—in Tunisia. This was in the standard form in which a quantity was also supplied to Britain (where they were known as the Lee) and by which name were, likewise, used in North Africa. M.3s were also employed by British Commonwealth forces in the Burma campaign of 1944; often in hybrid form, where they were commonly referred to as 'Lee/Grants', and were used also by the Australians for home defence. The other illustration shows a later production M.3 (with the longer 40 calibre 75-mm. gun) on issue to the U.S. Army training in Britain in 1942.

Sherman Medium Tank M.4

The Sherman is arguably one of the greatest tanks of World War II, even on numbers alone, because over 58,000 were built. The Sherman was a good straightforward design which proved adaptable, so that armament and armour modifications could be introduced to enable it to keep level with its opponents to the end of the war.

Design work on the M.4 as the definitive 75-mm. gun-armed medium tank to replace the medium M.3 model was commenced in March 1941. The prototype, known as T.6, was ready by September 1941 and after trials and minor design changes was approved for production commencing in early 1942.

Production of the M.4 in the numbers envisaged would have overrun the supply of Continental engines (as used in the M.3 and original M.4 designs) and so the use of alternative engines, already used in later models of the M.3, and others, was provided for. The most important of these were the General Motors 6046 twelve-cylinder diesel (two six-cylinder truck engines geared together) used in the M.4A2, the Ford GAA V-8 petrol engine, used in the M.4A3 and the Chrysler A.57 thirty-cylinder petrol engine used in the M.4A4.

Armament of the Sherman consisted originally of a 75-mm. M.3 gun (although short M.2 guns with counter-weights were provisionally fitted on some of the very first tanks built) with a coaxial 0.30-in. Browning machine-gun. In the front of the hull was a Browning machine-gun in a ball mounting and, beside it, two more Brownings, fixed to fire forwards only. The latter were eliminated after the early production vehicles. Most tanks in American use had a 0.50-in. Browning machine-gun mounted on a pintle on the turret for anti-aircraft use, although this weapon was not accurate and was commonly discarded in British-used tanks. Changes in the main armament of Shermans during the course of production included the 105-mm. howitzer in place of the 75-mm. gun, and the 76-mm. gun, a long high velocity cannon. These weapons were incorporated in a proportion of tanks during the course of production and some tanks supplied to Britain were modified to take the British 17-pr gun.

One illustration shows a side view of a typical Sherman armed with the 75-mm. gun and the other a 17-pr-equipped Sherman Vc of a British armoured regiment in Normandy in 1944.

Pershing Medium Tank M.26

Following the abandonment of heavy tanks in the U.S.A., attention was turned to the problem of mounting a 90-mm. gun in a medium tank. A series of experimental tanks was built between 1942 and 1944, trying out various suspension systems, transmissions and other components as well as various guns, including the 90-mm. This series culminated in the T.26E1 completed in January 1944. This tank with some modifications, including a muzzle brake on the 90-mm. gun and increased ammunition stowage, became the T.26E3. By this time the need for a better gun than the 76-mm., the best weapon fitted to M.4 Medium tanks, was recognized following combat experience in Normandy. There was, therefore, a demand for a 90-mm. gun tank but the T.26E3, now re-classified as a heavy tank was not yet considered battleworthy as it had been insufficiently tested. Twenty tanks out of the first batch to be built were, however, shipped to Europe for field trials and in January 1945 were now declared battleworthy. Allotted to the 3rd and 9th Armoured Divisions of the U.S. First Army, the tanks were named the General Pershing and standardized

as M.26. Production was by now well under way and 200 had been issued by the end of the war in Europe, although most arrived at the front too late to see action. Some that did—at Remagen on the Rhine—were some of the original Pershings issued to the 9th Armoured Division.

The M.26 weighed 46 (U.S.) tons. Besides the 90-mm. gun (53 calibres long) it had a coaxial 0.30-in. Browning machine-gun and another Browning in a ball-mounting in the hull glacis plate and a 0.50-in. anti-aircraft machine-gun on the turret top. The crew of five were protected by armour at a maximum of 102-mm.

The M.26's engine was a Ford Model GAF eight-cylinder V-form type of 500 b.h.p. and the transmission was Torquematic with three forward speeds, with the track drive from rear sprockets. Suspension was of the torsion bar type and a maximum speed of 30 m.p.h. could be attained.

Although arriving too late to see much action in World War II, the Pershing was the direct ancestor of a long line of post-war U.S. medium tanks.

A tank which received much publicity in the Allied press in 1941-42 was the American M.6 heavy tank. Sometimes shown crushing motor cars, the 50-ton M.6 was of spectacular appearance and, for its time, was a powerful tank.

Called for in 1940 as a heavy tank to complement the M.3 Medium, the first pilot model, out of several designed to test alternative forms of hull construction, transmission and power unit, was completed at the end of 1941. This model, T.1E2, had a cast hull and a torque converter transmission and was later standardized as Heavy Tank M.6. The T.1E3, which appeared slightly later, had a welded hull but was otherwise similar, and was standardized as M.6A1. The third to appear, T.1E1, was ready in 1943—this model had electric transmission and a cast hull. It was usually known later as M.6A2.

All models of this heavy tank were powered by a Wright G-200 radial nine-cylinder air-cooled engine of 800 b.h.p. which gave a maximum speed of about 22 m.p.h. The main armament consisted of a 3-in. gun (a modified anti-aircraft gun) with a coaxial 37-mm. gun in the turret. (The T.1E2 had also a 0.30-in. Browning machine-gun in a separate cupola on top and a 0.50-in. machine-gun on a high-angle mounting at the right rear of the turret.) Two 0.50-in. machine-guns were mounted in the front hull plate under the control of the co-driver and the driver was responsible for two (later one) fixed machine-guns. Armour was at a maximum of 100-mm. and a crew of six was carried.

Because of disagreement over the need for a heavy tank, the large orders originally envisaged were reduced drastically to one hundred and fifteen in September 1942 and then cancelled altogether at the end of the year, although there were subsequent experiments with 90-mm. and 105-mm. guns. Consequently, no more than forty of all variants of the M.6 series, including prototypes, were built. Apart from propaganda purposes, however, the programme had involved useful work, which was not wasted, on armour design, gun stabilizers and power traverse, horizontal volute spring suspension and transmissions, as all these features of the M6 were used in various later light and medium tanks.

The illustrations show the M.6 (T.1E2) and (below) the M.6A1.

Priest 105-mm. Howitzer Motor Carriage M.7

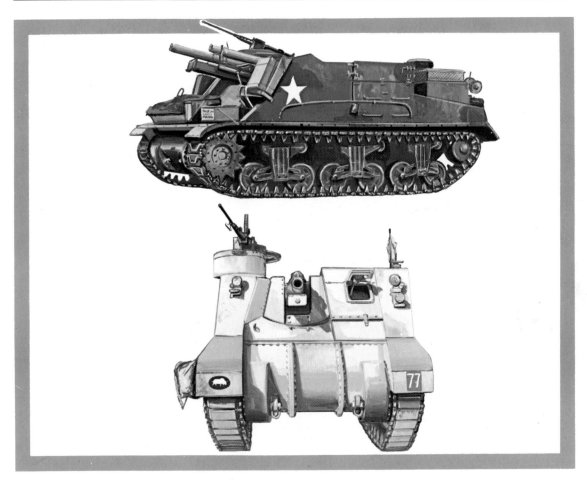

In action for the first time with British forces in North Africa, where it formed an important element in the self-propelled artillery available at the Alamein battle in October 1942, the Howitzer Motor Carriage M.7 became the main field artillery component in U.S. armoured divisions during World War II.

The decision to mount a 105-mm. field howitzer on the same chassis as the M.3 Medium Tank was taken in June 1941. Production began in April 1942, so that the first ninety vehicles for British use were delivered in Egypt in September. A Priest (as they were named by the British) belonging to 11th Regiment, Royal Horse Artillery (of 1st Armoured division), which received its first Priests on 10 September 1942, is shown in one of the illustrations. This vehicle has the earlier type of 3-piece noseplate.

The M.7 had the 105-mm. howitzer mounted to the right of the hull centre line to fire forwards, with a total traverse of 45 degrees. The driver sat at the left, and a characteristic dustbin-shaped 'pulpit' mounting for a 0.5-in. Browning machine-gun was at the right. The Continental nine-cylinder radial engine, drive train and suspension were all similar to those of the M.3 medium. Maximum speed was about 25 m.p.h. Armour was at a maximum thickness of 62 mm. although there was no overhead protection for the crew of seven, except for the driver.

A later, but generally similar, version of the M.7, the M.7B1, using M.4 Medium Tank components replaced the former in production from March 1944 onwards until the type was gradually replaced by the M.37 in the last months of the war.

The M.7 was used widely by field artillery units in U.S. armoured divisions from 1942 to 1945 in most theatres of war, including North West Europe. An M.7 in this area as it appeared in late 1944 is shown in one of the coloured views. After the North African campaign Priests continued in American and British use in the Sicilian and Italian campaigns which followed (and during which, incidentally, a 10-in. mortar was experimentally fitted in one). They were also employed by British troops in the Burma campaign and in the opening stages of the Normandy operations.

3-in. Gun Motor Carriage M.10 and 76-mm. Gun Motor Carriage M.18.

It was American philosophy in 1942 that enemy tanks should be engaged wherever possible by specialized 'tank destroyers', rather than by their own tanks. The characteristics required of a tank destroyer were a powerful gun and a good speed, even if these were attained at the expense of reduced protection for the crew. The Gun Motor Carriage M.10 was an adaptation of the M.4 Medium Tank chassis based on these principles. The powerful 3-in. gun was mounted in an open-top fully rotating turret on a modified M.4 tank hull with engines, transmission and suspension, equivalent to corresponding vehicles in the M.4 series. The maximum armour thickness was only 37-mm., although the side plates of the hull were, unlike those of the M.4, sloped to give better protection. The M.10 had twin General Motors diesel engines like the Medium Tank M.4A2, and the M.10A1 (externally similar to the M.10) had the Ford GAA eight-cylinder petrol engine, like the M.4A3. In either case, the maximum speed was 30 m.p.h.

Some M.10's and M.10A1's were supplied to the United Kingdom, and they were used by British and Commonwealth forces in Italy and North West Europe.

A British modification to a proportion of the vehicles received was the substitution of the 17-pr for the 3-in. gun.

The Gun Motor Carriage M.18 continued the idea behind the M.10 but on a more modern chassis which, because of its weight of around 19 tons with a high power/weight ratio, turned out to be the fastest tracked fighting vehicle of World War II. Up to 55 m.p.h. could be achieved.

After undergoing several changes in both armament and suspension, the M.18, later nicknamed Hellcat, in its final form consisted of a 76-mm. gun, 55 calibres long, mounted in a partly open top turret on a new chassis with torsion bar suspension, powered by a Continental nine-cylinder radial engine of 340 b.h.p. (400 b.h.p. engines in some). The driver sat at the left front of the hull and the co-driver at the right, with the three other crew members in the turret. The commander sat at the left side of the turret, where he was able to operate the 0.50-in. Browning machine-gun carried on a ring mounting on the turret top.

Between July and October 1944, 2,507 M.18's were built, and all went to the U.S. Army.

Tracked Landing Vehicle (Unarmored) Mark IV and Tracked Landing Vehicle (Armored) Mark IV

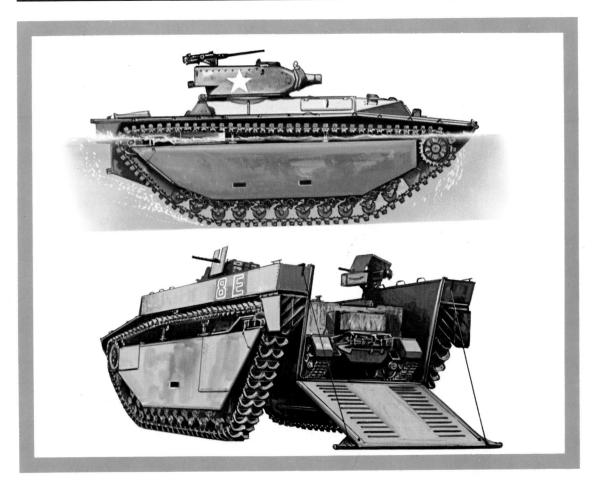

The great majority of amphibious cargo carriers used in World War II were built by the United States; neither her Allies nor her enemies, apart from Japan, paying very much attention to this class of vehicle.

The type was derived from an amphibian designed by Donald Roebling, intended for rescue work in hurricanes and the swampy Everglades region of Florida. A militarized version of Reobling's 1940 model was ordered as a Landing Vehicle Tracked for the U.S. Marine Corps and known as L.V.T.1. A greatly improved model, L.V.T.2, appeared in 1943. The next development, which finally became the L.V.T.3, had twin Cadillac engines in the pontoons at either side, so enabling a rear-loading ramp to be incorporated. The L.V.T.2, which had a single seven-cylinder Continental radial engine, was also modified to provide an unobstructed hold with a rear-loading ramp by having the engine moved forward, the result being known as L.V.T.4.

Armoured cargo and support versions of the L.V.T.'s were also developed, the L.V.T.(A)1 and L.V.T.(A)2, both having a similar chassis to the L.V.T.2, the former being enclosed, with an M.3 light tank turret (37-mm.

gun and 0.30-in. Browning machine-gun) mounted on the roof, the latter a cargo carrier only. The L.V.T.(A)4 was similar to the L.V.T.(A)1, except that a 75-mm. howitzer turret from the M.8 gun motor carriage was used.

All the L.V.T. series were propelled in water by means of their tracks, which on all except the original L.V.T.1 had W-shaped grousers added. The water speed for all models was between 6 and 7½ m.p.h. The L.V.T.1 had an unsprung suspension system, but all the later L.V.T.s used an interesting rubber torsion suspension. Each road wheel was mounted independently on an arm, the pivot of which was a hollow tube, fitted over a smaller tube attached to the hull. The space between the two tubes was filled with vulcanized rubber which, in resisting the movement of the tube-carrying road wheel, acted like a spring.

The production of L.V.T.s in the United States amounted to 1,225 L.V.T.1s, 3,413 L.V.T.2s and L.V.T.(A)2s, 509 L.V.T.(A)1s, 1,890 L.V.T.(A)4s and 8,438 L.V.T.4s. The L.V.T.3 appeared late in World War II and was first used in action in April 1945—2,962 were built, many of which saw service after the war.

Staghound I Armored Car (T.17E1) and Boarhound Armored Car (T.18E2)

British experience in the North African desert had shown that good use could be made of armoured cars in this kind of terrain and several American armoured car designs were started in 1941-42, prompted by British needs. The first of these were the T.17 and T.17E1 commenced in June 1941. Both rear-engined armoured cars, equipped with a 37-mm. gun turret (somewhat like that of the Grant medium tank) and generally alike in layout and appearance, the T.17 was a six-wheeled vehicle (6×6) by Ford and the T.17E1 was four-wheeled and designed by General Motors (Chevrolet Motor Car Division). Some 3, 760 T.17s and 3,500 T.17E1s were on order by June 1942, but in reviewing the overall production of armoured cars, the Special Armored Vehicle board decided to eliminate the T.17 on the grounds that it was too heavy.

The T.17E1, known in Britain as Staghound, was without a chassis as such, the automotive components being attached direct to the armoured hull. The power unit consisted of two six-cylinder G.M.C. Model 270 engines, each of 97 b.h.p., mounted at the rear and driving all four wheels through a Hydramatic (automatic) transmission. The turret carried a 37-mm.

gun and a 0.30-in. Browning machine-gun, mounted coaxially, and there was another Browning machine-gun in a ball mount in the glacis plate, controlled by the co-driver at the right. The driver, who enjoyed power steering, sat at the left. Hull armour was at a maximum of ⅞ inches (22-mm.), although the turret was mainly 1¼-1¾ inches thick.

Staghounds found useful employment as command vehicles at squadron and regimental headquarters, where their roominess and provision for a crew of five were advantages. A Staghound belonging to the regimental headquarters of a British armoured car regiment is shown in the illustration.

The heavy armoured car T.18E2 had all the characteristics required for open desert warfare to an even greater degree than the Staghound and, like it, unfortunately was ready only when the campaign in North Africa was over. It weighed over 26 (short) tons and was over 20 feet long, but the armament was only a 6-pr gun and two 0.30-in Browning machine-guns. Only 30 T.18E2s were built, all of them for British use, but none saw action.

Light Armored Car M.8 and Armored Utility Car M.20.

The best American armoured car of World War II, the T.22 was designed by the Ford Motor Co. in competition with other 6×4 and 4×4 projects by Studebaker and Fargo. Out of these and many other armoured car designs at this time only the T.17E1 and the T.22, which was completed in early 1942, modified as T.22E2 and standardized as M.8, remained to be produced in quantity after a critical survey had been carried out by the Special Armored Vehicle Board.

A six-wheeled, six-wheel-drive vehicle with a rear-mounted engine—the 110 b.h.p. six-cylinder Hercules JXD—the M.8 had a welded hull (armoured to a maximum of ¾-in.) and a circular cast turret with an open top. The armament consisted of a 37-mm. gun and a 0.30-in. Browning machine-gun in the turret with provision for a 0.50-in. heavy machine-gun to be mounted on the turret-top. With a four-speed gear-box, the maximum speed of the M.8 was 55 m.p.h. The car had a four-man crew.

The Armoured Utility Car M.20 was a companion vehicle to the M.8, to which it was mechanically identical. Intended as a command vehicle or armoured personnel or cargo carrier, it differed from the M.8 in having no turret and a square, raised centre section of the hull. This was open-topped and was surmounted by a ring-mounting for a 0.50-in. machine-gun. The M.20 could carry up to six men, according to function.

The M.8 (but not the M.20) was also supplied to the United Kingdom for use by the British and Commonwealth armies. Named Greyhound in British service, the M.8's characteristics were summarized as having a magnificent cross-country performance; being hard to reverse; difficult to protect against mines (the thin hull floor armour—⅛ inch to ¼ inch—was often reinforced by sandbags) and the useful advantage in a reconnaissance vehicle of being able to cross Class 9 bridges.

The illustrations show an M.8 of the U.S. Army in North West Europe (the fifteenth vehicle in C Troop of a reconnaissance unit) with impedimenta as carried in a campaign, and an M.20 in 'parade ground' condition.

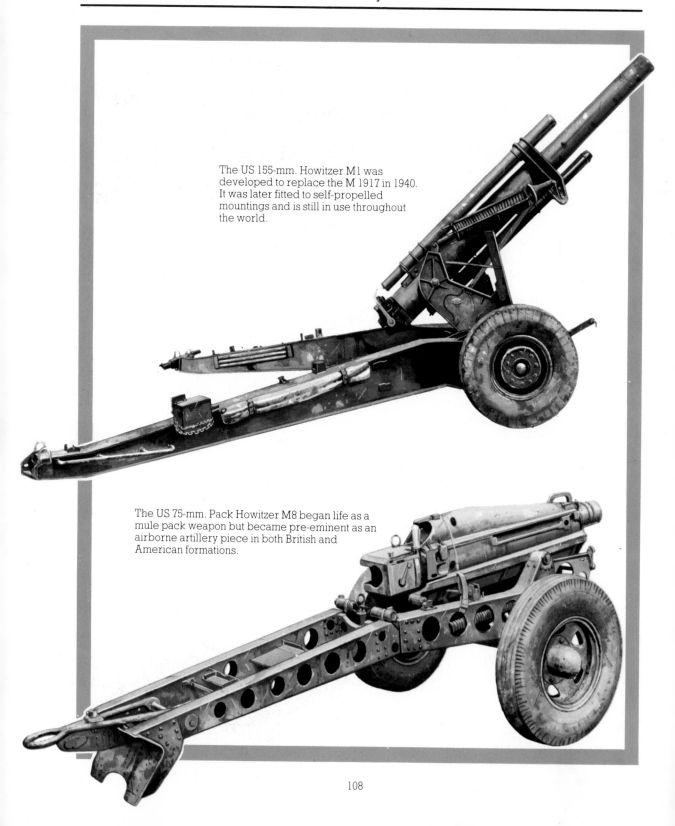

The US 155-mm. Howitzer M1 was developed to replace the M 1917 in 1940. It was later fitted to self-propelled mountings and is still in use throughout the world.

The US 75-mm. Pack Howitzer M8 began life as a mule pack weapon but became pre-eminent as an airborne artillery piece in both British and American formations.

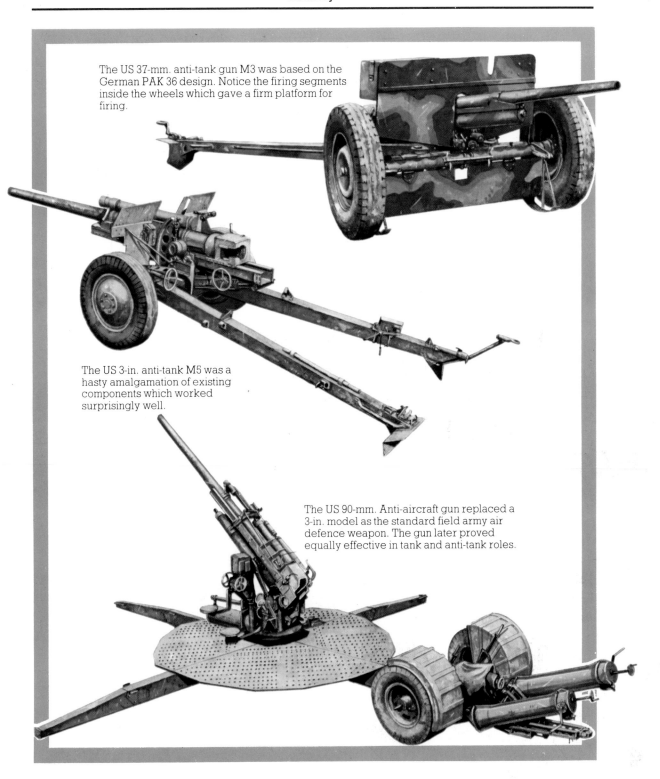

The US 37-mm. anti-tank gun M3 was based on the German PAK 36 design. Notice the firing segments inside the wheels which gave a firm platform for firing.

The US 3-in. anti-tank M5 was a hasty amalgamation of existing components which worked surprisingly well.

The US 90-mm. Anti-aircraft gun replaced a 3-in. model as the standard field army air defence weapon. The gun later proved equally effective in tank and anti-tank roles.

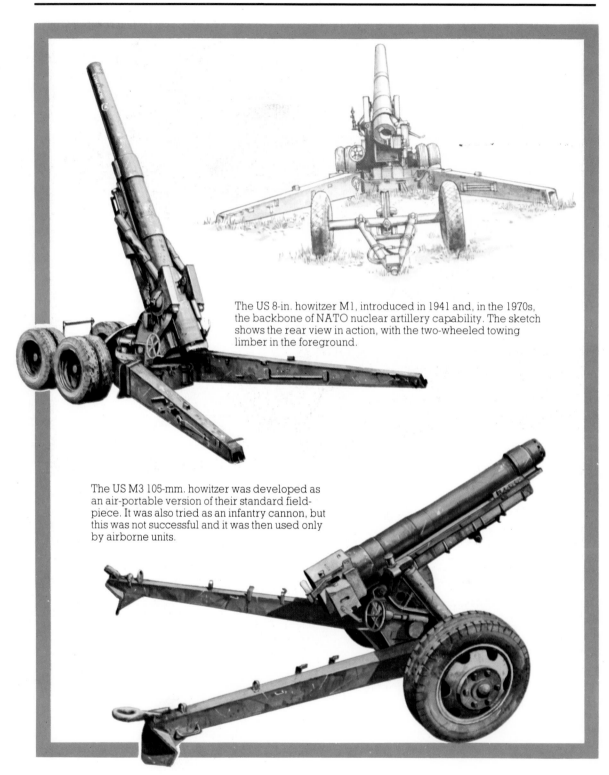

The US 8-in. howitzer M1, introduced in 1941 and, in the 1970s, the backbone of NATO nuclear artillery capability. The sketch shows the rear view in action, with the two-wheeled towing limber in the foreground.

The US M3 105-mm. howitzer was developed as an air-portable version of their standard field-piece. It was also tried as an infantry cannon, but this was not successful and it was then used only by airborne units.

The only heavy armoured car to be employed by the U.S.S.R. in the Second World War, the BA-32 was a direct successor – and easily recognisable as such – to the BA-10 which first went into mass production in 1930. Very typical of their era (armoured cars of similar type were built in Britain, Germany and the U.S.A.), the BA-10 and BA-32 were built on GAZ six-wheeled lorry chassis, the GAZ being a Russian version of a Ford design. The use of a normal front-engined chassis of this kind largely dictated the armoured car layout, so that the driver was behind the engine, with a co-driver's machine-gun position beside him, and the turret was located over the rear wheels. The turrets used in this BA-10/BA-32 series were those of

contemporary tanks and the armament ranged from a 37-mm. gun and coaxial machine-gun, in early versions, to the 45-mm. gun and machine-gun in the version (BA-32-2) shown in the illustrations. The armoured hull was of riveted construction in the early verions, but welding later came increasingly into use and in the final version the hull sides were more sloping and the roof at the rear was lowered, together with the turret, so that the 45-mm. gun only just cleared the part of the hull over the driver's head.

To improve its performance over snow or soft ground the rear wheels of the BA-32 could be fitted with tracks, as shown in one of the illustrations.

BT-7 ('Fast Tank')

The most important Soviet tank numerically in 1939, the BT-7 was the last in a series developed from an almost exact copy of the American Christie M-1931 tank.

Two Christie tanks were imported from the United States in 1931 and given searching tests in the U.S.S.R. which were obviously satisfactory, because they were followed by the manufacture, in a remarkably short time, of the first vehicles built under licence. They were adapted slightly and simplified to meet Soviet production requirements but even the power plant – a Liberty V twelve-cylinder modified aero engine – was built in the U.S.S.R. After use in service, the series was developed through a number of models up to the BT-7, which first went into production in 1935. The type had the special Russian classification of Bystrochodnij Tank ('Fast Tank').

Although superior to earlier models in engine power, armour and armament, the BT-7 retained the salient Christie features of high speed, both on and off tracks, and good cross-country running ability. These characteristics were due mainly to the high power/weight ratio of over 30 h.p./ton and the Christie suspension system, consisting of four large-diameter road wheels each side, independently mounted at the end of leading or trailing swing arms, controlled by long coil springs. The springs were mounted between the inner and outer hull side plates. Transmission from the engine mounted at the rear was to track-drive sprockets at the back. On wheels, the BT-7 had a top speed of 45 m.p.h., but even on tracks the maximum was 33 m.p.h.

The BT-7 in its later standardised form had armament consisting of a 45-mm. gun and a coaxial 7.62-mm. machine-gun. In some cases, there was a second machine-gun in a ball mounting in the rear of the turret, which was mainly of welded construction. Earlier models, however (like the BT-7-1, shown on wheels in one of the illustrations), retained the older cylindrical riveted turret of the BT-5. The original Liberty engine had, in the BT-7, been replaced by a 450 h.p. twelve-cylinder V-type of different design.

Medium Tank T-28C

Believed to have been inspired by contemporary British and German designs (the A.6 Medium and the so-called 'Gross traktor' series, respectively) the T-28 was the first Russian-built medium tank to be accepted for service with the Red Army.

Designed at the Kirov Plant at Leningrad, the first prototype of the T-28 was tested during 1932. After modifications this model was put into production. Development was continued through several models and manufacture was continued until 1939 with the final standard model, T-28C, which is shown in the illustrations.

The T-28C shared the same layout and characteristics of the earlier models, but a newer, more powerful version of the 76.2-mm. main gun (of calibre L/26) was used. Also included in the main turret was a machine-gun in a ball mounting. The two auxiliary turrets, one either side of the driver, had one machine-gun each so that in the frontal assaults for

which the T-28 was intended, a bewildering volume of fire could be maintained. The frontal armour of the T-28C was likewise improved, to a maximum of 80-mm., although it is likely that this was of limited distribution.

The driver's and fighting compartments of the T-28 (occupied by the crew of six) were in the front half of the tank and the engine compartment was at the rear, the transmission being to rear drive sprockets. The engine used was the M-17L (a Russian version of the American Liberty aero engine) twelve-cylinder V of 500 h.p.: this gave a top speed of about 20 m.p.h.

Although the specification of the T-28 does not appear bad on paper, the design was found to be inadequate even in the Finnish campaign and when in 1941 these tanks came up against German armour their tall silhouette (with auxiliary turrets which were virtually useless in open warfare) and relatively thin rear and side armour made them easy victims.

This imposing but thinly-armoured heavy tank was one of the last manifestations of the fashion set by the British A1.E1 'Independent' tank of 1926.

The idea behind the A1.E1 was that by providing the tank with a multiplicity of turrets, so that fire could be brought to bear on all sides at once, combined with mobility, independent missions could be undertaken without support by other arms. Although Russian tactical ideas may not necessarily have coincided with those of the British, a Soviet tank on the same theme as the A1.E1 (which was experimental only) was put into service about 1931. This was the T-32 and it was followed in 1933 by the T-35, which continued in production until 1939, although a total of only twenty to thirty was built.

Like its British progenitor, the T-35 had five turrets; a large turret mounting the main armament and four subsidiary turrets grouped round it. The main turret mounted a 76.2-mm. gun and one machine-gun in a ball mounting in the turret face; two of the auxiliary turrets (the front right and rear left) mounted 45-mm. guns and the other two small turrets had one machine-gun each.

Early versions of the tank had 37-mm. guns instead of 45-mm. and there were various modifications to the armament (sometimes involving the removal of the two machine-gun turrets) in the later years of the T-35's existence. Armour protection was to a front hull maximum of 30-mm. on early models and 35-mm. on later versions.

Powered by a 500 h.p. twelve-cylinder V model M-17 M engine situated in the rear half of the hull, the 45-ton T-35 had a maximum road speed of 18 m.p.h. The cross-country speed was given as 12 m.p.h. and it is likely that, because of its length (32 ft), this could be maintained by the T-35 better than most of its contemporaries. The clutch and brake steering system was said to have been unsatisfactory, however.

Tanks of this type were used in the 1939 Finnish campaign, where they were not very successful, and a number were also intended for use against the Germans in Poland in 1941 where, however, they ran out of fuel before being engaged.

The illustrations show the second model of the T-35, fitted with a frame wireless aerial on the turret.

Light Tank T-26B

The T-26 was the Russian-built version of the Vickers-Armstrong 6-ton Tank, fifteen of which were ordered from the United Kingdom in 1930. The original Vickers tank was available in two models, one with two turrets, side by side, and the other with a single large turret. The original T-26s built under licence were almost identical to their British-made prototypes. Both twin- and single-turret versions were manufactured in the Soviet Union, but from about 1933 development of the 6-ton type of tank was concentrated on the single-turret model, in which a larger gun could be installed.

Production of the T-26 ran through until 1939, the final standard version being the T-26S (usually known outside the U.S.S.R. as T-26C). This differed externally from earlier models in the increased use of welded armour, with sloping hull plates and a turret of more streamlined appearance than hitherto. Turrets of this later type were in some cases used to replace those of earlier pattern on earlier models of the T-26, T-26Bs with the new turret are shown in the illustrations.

Apart from this relatively minor change, the T-26 remained both in mechanical specification and general appearance very close to its prototype, the Vickers-

Armstrong 6-ton tank. The engine, an Armstrong-Siddeley eight-cylinder 90 h.p., air-cooled type, built under licence, was situated at the rear, the transmission being led forwards to drive front sprockets. The gearbox (beside the driver's feet) had five forward speeds and steering was of the clutch and brake type. The suspension was of the simple robust type designed by Vickers and consisted of two groups of four bogie wheels each side, sprung on quarter-elliptic leaf springs. The crew compartment was in the centre of the vehicle with the driver at the right.

In its armament the T-26B and later Soviet models were greatly improved over the Vickers 6-ton in that the short 47-mm. gun was replaced by a long 45-mm. L/46 gun of much higher muzzle velocity. There was also a coaxial machine-gun and in some cases a second machine-gun in the turret rear.

T-26s of all models were an important factor in the building up of the tank strength of the U.S.S.R. in the 1930s, and although mass production ceased in 1939, they were used in action against the Finns in 1939-40 and even against the Germans in 1941, although phased out of service soon afterwards.

The KV heavy tank (the initials stand for Klementy Voroshilov, a Marshal of the Soviet Union) was the third of a trio of designs in 1938 for a modern type to take the place of the old and unsatisfactory T-35.

The first two models (T-100 and SMK) both had two turrets (reduced at the drawing-board stage from three, at the suggestion of Stalin) and the other, which later was evolved as the KV I, had only one turret. It was, again, Stalin's influence that led to the choice of this model.

The KV I was designed as a heavy tank to enjoy the maximum protection from contemporary armour-piercing weapons coupled with an effective armament, in which the total weight should not become excessive and so cut down on mobility. A prototype of this tank was completed in September 1939 and several pre-production vehicles were in use on the Finnish front before the end of the year.

The main features of the layout of the KV I were a centrally mounted turret containing a 76.2-mm. gun and two machine-guns (one coaxial, one in the rear face); the driver's compartment at the front with a hull machine-gun position to the left of the driver, and a rear-mounted diesel engine. This was a V-form twelve-cylinder power unit of 550 h.p. which drove rear sprockets via a five-speed gearbox. The tracks were exceptionally wide – 27½-in. – and this helped to keep ground pressure down to little more than that of the very much lighter BT-7. Armour protection was on a generous basis, to around 100-mm. on the front of the hull and turret.

During the course of production of the KV series, improvements in both armour and armament were introduced, some tanks having a longer calibre 76.2-mm. gun and others, like the KV IB (shown in the illustrations), with both hull and turret armour supplemented by the addition of extra plates. In the case of the KV IB (the suffix was added by the Germans, incidentally, as a means of identifying this model) the additional plates were welded on to the glacis and driver's plates but bolted on to the hull and turret sides. The bolt heads were a particularly prominent feature on the turret.

Although inevitably outmoded as the War progressed, the KV I proved to be a very good design which was later used for the basis of the Stalin tank.

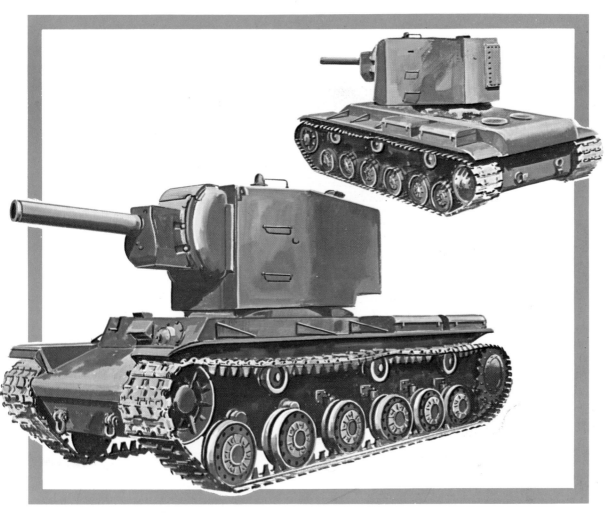

First appearing in early 1940, this massive and cumbersome vehicle was an 'artillery tank' version of the KV I. A 152-mm. howitzer (122-mm. calibre in the very earliest models) mounted in a high, square turret took the place of the normal 76.2-mm. gun turret. This turret had a 360-degree traverse but it weighed around 12 tons and the bearings were badly designed, so that it could only be traversed when the tank was on level ground. The increase in all-up weight of about 10 tons without any increase in power, coupled with much higher centre of gravity, inevitably decreased mobility, although in any case the gun could not be fired on the move.

KV IIs used the same chassis as KV Is and the later versions of the former (known as KV IIB by the Germans) had the wider tracks of the KV IB as well as a slightly different turret and gun mounting.

The KV IIs had some success when employed in the assault on the Mannerheim Line in Finland but were found to be virtually useless when meeting the German invasion of Russia in the Summer of 1941 and they do not appear to have been used after 1941. Since the chassis were identical with those of the KV I, however, it seems likely that most KV IIs which survived were converted to KV Is.

The tank which had the greatest impact on the course of the Second World War was probably the Russian T-34. Although not the best in a mechanical sense, and the T-34 had several shortcomings in design, this Russian tank was nevertheless one of the most effective fighting vehicles of all time and its influence is still felt.

The most remarkable feature of the T-34 when it first appeared was the extremely effective use of sloped armour plates for the hull. This fact, coupled with a good gun (the 76.2-mm. L/30.5 in the first production model) and a diesel engine of 500 h.p., which ensured good mobility, added up to make a tank which had a traumatic effect on the Wehrmacht.

The suspension was of the usual Christie type, with large road wheels on pivot arms controlled by long coil springs. The track design was unusual, though, in that the wide (19-in.) plates were held together by pins which were retained in place only by plates, attached to the hull, which pushed back the heads of any projecting pins as they passed.

The twelve-cylinder V-form diesel engine of the T-34 was tried out in the BT-7M, the last of the BT series, and performed well in the T-34, although the transmission system at first gave trouble – faults probably of manufacture rather than design, though.

The hull of the T-34 in its early versions was 45-mm. thick at the front and 40-mm. at the sides and was divided internally by one bulkhead separating the engine from the crew compartment. The driver sat at the front with, beside him, the co-driver, who operated a machine-gun mounted in the glacis plate. The turret, mounted near the front of the hull roof, was protected mainly on a 45-mm. basis on early T-34s, and the 76.2-mm. gun shared a mounting with a 7.62-mm. machine-gun.

The gun mantlet in the first T-34 production model was of the external type, cast, and of a form (when used on the Sturmgeschütz III) known to the Germans as 'saukopf' (pig's head). This early T-34 (T 34/76A) is shown in the illustrations.

Medium Tanks T-34 ('T-34/76B') and T-34/85

The immense superiority of the T-34 over its opponents when it first appeared in action in 1941 was countered by the Germans with the introduction of the Panther and Tiger, and by up-gunning the PzKpfw IV. Nevertheless, successive improvements in the armament and protection of the T-34 kept it in the forefront of medium tanks throughout the rest of the war.

The original production version of the T-34, the T-34/76A, as it became known outside the Soviet Union, had a turret design which was unsatisfactory in some respects. This was replaced in the T-34/76B by a new turret incorporating a 76.2-mm. gun with a length of 41.2 calibres (compared with the earlier gun's 30.5 calibres) and increased muzzle velocity. Vision arrangements were improved and the 'pig's head' type of mantlet was replaced by a bolted one of more angular shape in which the gun was mounted relatively higher. The earlier turrets of Model B were of rolled plate, welded, but during 1942 a cast version was introduced and this pattern is shown in the illustration.

Good as it was, it became necessary to increase the hitting power of the T-34 and during the summer of 1943, A. A. Morozov, who had taken over as chief designer from M. I. Koshkin, who died in 1940, redesigned the tank to accept a new turret armed with an 85-mm. gun. The gun was an adaptation of a pre-war anti-aircraft gun and was in a turret designed for the KV-85 heavy tank, so, once more, introducing standardization between the two classes of Russian tank. Later, though, this turret was re-designed and the second model of the T-34/85, using the new turret is shown in the illustration in this book.

The T-34/85's roomier turret enabled a five-man crew to be used and the protection was increased to a maximum of 75-mm. at the front. The main essentials of all T-34's remained, however, including the V-12 cylinder diesel engine of 500 h.p. driving rear sprockets and the Christie suspension of large road wheels on pivot arms controlled by long coil springs. Although many improvements had been introduced since 1940, the T-34 was still basically a simple and rugged but effective design, well suited to mass production. Nearly 40,000 T-34s of all types were built during World War II.

Heavy Tank KV-85 and Self-propelled Gun SU 85

The need to improve the armament of the KV-1 heavy tank was emphasized during the great battle of Kursk in 1943, in which the Soviet tanks encountered the German Tiger tanks in appreciable numbers. The 85-mm. gun in a new turret was fitted to the KV-1 in that year and the first of the new tanks, designated KV-85, were in action by the Autumn of 1943. The new combination was roughly equivalent to the German Tiger I (although more lightly armoured) and the Russians took the opportunity of reworking existing KV-Is to the new standard in order to make available quickly larger numbers of tanks capable of taking on the Tiger on equal terms. By Russian standards only small numbers of KV-85s were built – but the design was used as the basis of the Stalin tank which succeeded the KV series.

Roughly at the time the KV-85 appeared in service in 1943 and when a heavy tank with a more powerful gun than the 85-mm. was already envisaged, the SU-85 was designed. This SU (the initials stand for Samachodnya

Ustanovka – self-propelled [gun] mounting) was intended as a 'tank hunter' and carried the high velocity 85-mm. gun in a mounting with limited traverse in a low (and hence less conspicuous) well-armoured hull on the T-34 chassis. This device, of using a standard (or sometimes, obsolescent) chassis to mount a heavier gun and, at the same time, achieve better protection and/or mobility than with the same weapon on a tank, was widely used by the Germans in World War II.

Often used in conjunction with T-34/76s, the SU-85 was in production from about the end of 1943 for about a year, when it gradually began to be replaced by the SU-100, with a more powerful gun, which used the same chassis and which was similar in appearance. Another widely used self-propelled gun on the T-34 chassis was the SU-122, a 122-mm. low velocity howitzer, which was in service from early 1943 onwards.

The Josef Stalin or JS-II heavy tank with its long 122-mm. gun was one of the most powerful tanks to go into service with any army in World War II.

A tank which traced its ancestry directly back to the KV series, the JS-II was another product of the design team headed by General Z. A. Kotin. Taking the KV-85 as a base, the best points were retained but others, including the suspension and transmission, were redesigned. A two-stage planetary transmission, combined with an improved engine led to better manoeuvrability and overall performance. At the same time, the opportunity was taken of rearranging the internal layout in a more compact form, allowing for armour increases while decreasing the total weight compared with KV-85.

The earliest JS tanks had the same 85-mm. gun as the KV. This was then replaced by a 100-mm. weapon and then, finally, by the 122-mm. gun. As this gun needed a wider turret ring, the hull at that point had to be extended out over the tracks each side but to avoid increasing the height, the top run of the track was lowered, although in most other respects the torsion bar suspension of the JS was similar to that of the KVs.

Known as JS-I or JS-122, the first 122-mm. gun-armed Stalin tanks entered service in late 1943. The JS-II which followed was generally similar but had the hull redesigned to give greater protection, notably in the better slope on the glacis plate.

The 122-mm. gun on the JS-II had a 7.62-mm. machine-gun as a coaxial weapon. The tank was served by a crew of four. The combat weight was 45 tons and with a 600 b.h.p. twelve-cylinder V diesel engine had a top speed of 23 m.p.h. Armour was at a maximum thickness of 120-mm.

Over 2,000 JS-IIs were produced during the war, before being superseded by the even better JS-III, which became one of the most formidable tanks of the post-war years.

Two powerful self-propelled guns based on the Stalin heavy tank chassis, the JSU-122 and JSU-152 both entered service in 1944. Superseding similar weapons mounted on the earlier KV chassis (known as SU-122 and SU-152) to which they bore a strong resemblance, these two self-propelled guns had a better mechanical performance and, among other detail improvements, improved fire control arrangements.

The 122-mm. gun used in the earlier JSU-122s (one of which is shown in the illustration) was 45 calibres long and had a range of over 14,000 yards. Later models had a 43-calibre gun with a muzzle brake. The 152-mm. gun (29 calibres long) of the JSU-152 was a howitzer with a range of well over 9,000 yards. The ammunition (weighing 96 lb for high explosive and 107 lb per round for armour piercing) was so bulky, however, that only twenty rounds could be carried.

Carrying a crew of four (five if the vehicle was fitted with radio) the two JSUs were mechanically the same as their heavy tank counterparts and had much the same performance. This was important, because they were generally employed integrally with heavy tank regiments equipped with JS tanks.

Light Armoured Car BA-64

Armoured car development in the Soviet Union in World War II was very limited indeed because, apart from improvements to the two main pre-war designs, only one new model appeared. This was the BA-64, which went into production in 1942. A light armoured scout car with 4-wheel drive, said to have been inspired by the German SdKfz 222, to which it bore a slight resemblance, the BA-64 had a crew of two – the driver and the commander, who had a small open top multi-sided turret equipped with a machine-gun. This was normally a 7.62-mm. weapon, mounted in the turret face, or on top for anti-aircraft use, but alternatively a heavy 14.5-mm. machine-gun on a pintle mount could be carried.

Weighing about 2½ tons, the BA-64 was powered by a four-cylinder 50 b.h.p. GAZ petrol engine, which gave it a maximum speed of 31 m.p.h.

KT (Winged Tank) and Self-propelled Gun SU-76

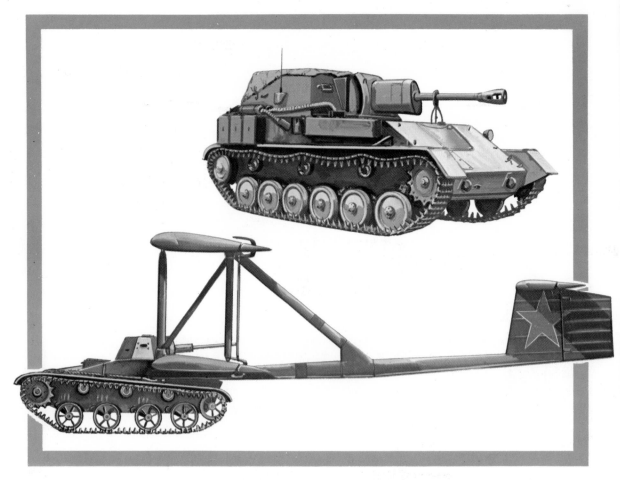

By the end of 1942, the Russians were already beginning to regard light tanks as obsolete and although the type was developed from the T-40 of 1941 through the T-60 and T-70 to the T-80 of 1943, production of light tanks was tailed off in that year and had ceased before the war ended.

The Russians also gave some consideration to the potential of the light tank as an airborne vehicle. One of the most interesting tank experiments by any country in World War II was the Russian design for a Kyrliatyi Tank (KT) or 'winged tank'.

This design, by a team led by O. Antonov, consisted of a T-60 light tank, more or less in standard form, to which biplane wings, twin booms and a tail assembly were attached. These aerodynamic structures were made of wood, mainly, it seems, because of the shortage of aircraft alloys for experiments of this kind. Rudimentary flying controls were led from the wings and tail to the tank, which formed the 'fuselage' of the machine.

The first test flight took place in 1942 and was curtailed only because of a fault in the engines of the towing aircraft. The winged tank apparently performed satisfactorily, but eventually the project had to be cancelled because of a shortage of four-engined towing aircraft.

The successor to the T-60 light tank was the T-70. Before production ceased it had already been decided to utilize the T-70 chassis as the basis of a self-propelled mounting for the 76.2-mm. anti-tank gun.

The vehicle which emerged, the SU-76, used automotive and running gear similar to that of the T-70, although an extra road wheel each side was added to accommodate the longer hull needed as a self-propelled mounting.

The 76.2-mm. gun, 41.5 calibres long, was mounted at the rear in an open-topped compartment with a total traverse of 32 degrees. The relatively light armour and absence of overhead protection made the SU-76 less suitable as an anti-tank vehicle once the gun began to be outranged by more powerful German weapons. It was replaced by the SU-85 as an anti-tank vehicle, therefore, and switched to the infantry support role.

The SU-76 shown in the illustration is one of the earlier production vehicles.

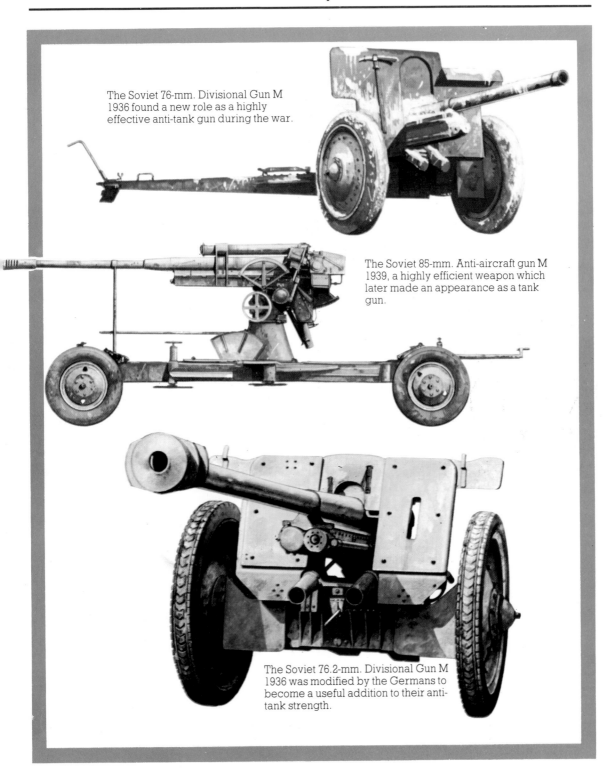

The Soviet 76-mm. Divisional Gun M 1936 found a new role as a highly effective anti-tank gun during the war.

The Soviet 85-mm. Anti-aircraft gun M 1939, a highly efficient weapon which later made an appearance as a tank gun.

The Soviet 76.2-mm. Divisional Gun M 1936 was modified by the Germans to become a useful addition to their anti-tank strength.

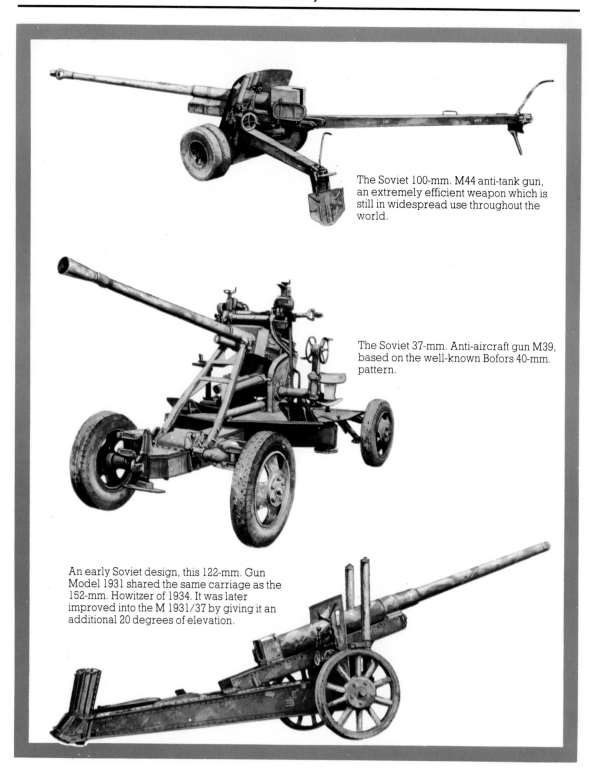

The Soviet 100-mm. M44 anti-tank gun, an extremely efficient weapon which is still in widespread use throughout the world.

The Soviet 37-mm. Anti-aircraft gun M39, based on the well-known Bofors 40-mm. pattern.

An early Soviet design, this 122-mm. Gun Model 1931 shared the same carriage as the 152-mm. Howitzer of 1934. It was later improved into the M 1931/37 by giving it an additional 20 degrees of elevation.

This book is based upon material first published by Blandford Press in TANKS OF THE BLITZKRIEG ERA 1939-41 and TANKS AND OTHER ARMOURED FIGHTING VEHICLES 1942-45 by B.T. White and illustrated by John W. Wood and in ARTILLERY IN COLOUR 1920-1963 by Ian Hogg and illustrated by Peter Sarson and Tony Bryan. The publishers wish to thank Michael Bowers Editions for assistance in the editorial preparation of this volume.